Dear Little Me

Embracing Our ADHD—We Were Never Too
Much, Never Not Enough

Patrycja Marta Jerushalmy

COPYRIGHT

DEDICATION

DEAR LITTLE ME...

To the little girl who always felt too much,

moved too fast,

and dreamed too big...

I see you now.

I see how your mind raced ahead of your words,

how your hands couldn't stay still,

how you felt everything so deeply it almost hurt.

I see how hard you tried to fit into a world that didn't understand you,

how you silenced parts of yourself to be what they wanted.

You wondered, why am I like this?

Why can't I be normal?

I want you to know:

You were never broken.

The things they called "too much" were never flaws.

Your energy was power,

your curiosity was brilliance,

your emotions were a gift—

but no one told you.

They only told you to slow down, to sit still, to focus.

They didn't know that your mind was a universe,

bursting with ideas, stories, and dreams too big for neat little boxes.

I am here now, Little Me.

I know what you didn't.

I know why you struggled to finish things that weren't exciting.

Why you felt lost in a sea of expectations you couldn't meet.

Why you were exhausted by the effort of keeping up,

holding it in,

masking the whirlwind inside you.

It was never your fault.

You weren't lazy.

You weren't careless.

You weren't failing.

You had ADHD.

No one saw it,

but I do.

And now, I will fight for you.

I will love you the way you always needed.

I will let you run, dream, and be wild.

I will honor your creativity,

your passions,

and your need for space to be exactly who you are.

I will never tell you to be less.

Because you were always enough.

And now?

We are finally free.

With love,

Me. 🤍

TABLE OF CONTENTS

WHO THIS BOOK IS REALLY FOR

Maybe it's your brain.

Maybe it's your child's.

Maybe it's someone you love and just don't understand yet.

If ADHD touches your life, you belong here.

This isn't about diagnosis or labels.

It's about recognition.

About finally seeing the whole picture.

This book is especially for:

• **PARENTS** trying to help their ADHD kids thrive without losing their minds

• **PARTNERS & FRIENDS** wanting to support someone they love, even when it's messy

- **TEACHERS & EDUCATORS** who want to understand the behavior beneath the surface

- **TEENS & ADULTS** who've spent years wondering why things that seem "easy" just aren't

- **ENTREPRENEURS & CREATIVES** with big ideas and brutal burnout

- **ANYONE** who's tired of shallow tips, shame cycles, and feeling misunderstood

If you've ever thought:

"Why do I keep getting in my own way when I know I'm capable of more?"

or

"How do I help someone I love without making them feel broken?"

This is your book.

WHY I WROTE
THIS BOOK

I never thought I'd write a book.

Not because I lacked ideas—my ADHD brain is a popcorn machine of brilliance—

but because finishing things? That's the battle.

I lived in loops.

New projects, huge energy, shiny excitement—

then crash, shame, and self-doubt.

Perfectionism whispered: *"Start over. Make it better. Don't mess it up."*

So I kept rewriting my life in my head and never quite on paper.

But life doesn't wait for perfect.

It cracked me open—hard.

And in that mess, I stopped pretending I needed to be fixed.

I just needed to be understood.

And I knew I wasn't alone.

This book started as a promise to my son—

that I would show up, unmasked.

It became a promise to myself—

that I would stop hiding.

Now, it's a promise to you.

If you've ever felt like too much or not enough,

if you've ever struggled to finish what you start,

if you've ever felt brilliant *and* broken at the same time—

this book is for you.

READ THIS FIRST (IF YOU'RE ADHD AND TIRED OF EVERY OTHER BOOK)

Let's get one thing out of the way:

This isn't a textbook.

This isn't a productivity guide full of tips you'll forget.

And it's definitely not another *"just try harder"* workbook.

This is a map, a mirror, and a megaphone for your ADHD brain.

It's built for people who feel too much, think fast, crash hard, and never fit the mold—

and who are done pretending they ever could.

You don't need more advice.

You need something that speaks your language.

HERE'S HOW THIS BOOK WORKS

Part 1: The Story

Real life. No lectures.

You'll walk through undiagnosed childhood, chaotic adulthood, parenting struggles, and the moment everything finally clicked.

If you've ever felt like you were surviving without a manual—this is your page one.

Part 2: The Science

This is where we decode the *why*.

Why you freeze. Why you feel too much. Why time doesn't feel real.

We'll break down the actual brain wiring behind:

- Executive dysfunction

- Dopamine loops

- Emotional dysregulation

- Sensory overwhelm

- Sleep spirals

- Rejection sensitivity

- Trauma overlap

- And the shame nobody sees

This part is not about fixing you—

it's about finally understanding you.

Part 3: The Tools

Here's where things get real.

We'll match every brain pattern with tools that actually fit your rhythms.

You'll learn how to:

- Start without force

- Reclaim energy

- Stop time from melting

- Work with your flavor of ADHD

- Build recovery, not just productivity

- Regulate your body and brain

- Create your own self-trust rituals

These aren't hacks.

These are systems that move with you, not against you.

ONE MORE THING

If your mind feels like a double-edged sword—

creative yet chaotic, brilliant but stuck—

this book was built for you.

You don't need to be fixed.

You just need the right frame.

This book is written for ADHD brains—

meaning you'll find rhythm over rules.

Some sentences flow like conversation.

Some break into breath-sized lines.

It's not an editing glitch—

it's how my brain thinks,

and maybe how yours does too.

Welcome.

Let's go.

A NOTE BEFORE YOU BEGIN

This book is a personal story.

It reflects my lived experience with ADHD—my own, and my son's.

I'm not a doctor, therapist, or medical professional.

Nothing in these pages is medical advice, diagnosis, treatment, or instruction.

What I'm sharing here helped me, or helped us.

If something resonates—beautiful.

If something doesn't—leave it. No pressure.

Every brain is different.

You are the expert on your own body, your own rhythm, your own life.

If you're thinking about making changes to your care, medication, or mental health plan, please talk to your doctor or care team first. They know you. This book doesn't.

You'll find the full disclaimer at the back of the book.

But I wanted you to know—right here, from the start—

I'm here to share. That's all.

Thanks for being here with me.

Part 1

MY ADHD ORIGIN STORY — FROM CHAOS TO CLARITY

REAL LIFE. NO TIPS. JUST THE UNFILTERED TRUTH OF WHAT IT'S LIKE TO LIVE, PARENT, CRASH, AND RISE WITH ADHD.

Chapter 1

BORN TO BE "TOO MUCH"

GROWING UP UNDIAGNOSED & MISUNDERSTOOD

From the moment I could talk, I talked too much, moved too much, asked too many questions, and challenged every rule.

I was a whirlwind of energy in a world that wanted stillness.

My earliest memories are filled with teachers scolding me for speaking out of turn, and my parents sighing as I dashed around the house like a pinball.

"Why can't you just sit still? Why can't you focus?" they'd ask.

But I didn't have an answer.

Keeping still felt unbearable.

My mind raced with thoughts too big to hold inside.

Looking back, my ADHD was obvious.

But in a time and place where few understood it, I was simply labeled as:

- *Too talkative*

- *Too impulsive*

- *Too scattered*

- *Too curious*

I tried my best to fit in—

but it was like trying to trap a tornado in a glass bottle.

It never worked.

And it only left me feeling more broken.

I remember sitting at my desk, staring at the clock while my teacher droned on about equations I had no interest in.

My legs bounced beneath the table.

My fingers tapped a restless rhythm.

I'd finished my work five minutes ago, but instead of praise for being quick, I was scolded for disrupting the class.

"Patrycja, can't you just sit still for once?"

The other kids snickered.

My cheeks burned with embarrassment.

Saying *"I can't help it"* never felt like a valid excuse.

So, I learned to hide it.

I bit my lip when I wanted to interrupt.

I forced my hands to stay still when they ached to move.

I tried to act normal.

But it was exhausting.

I wasn't just pretending to be someone else—

I was erasing who I truly was, one piece at a time.

By the time I was a teenager, I had mastered the art of masking:

knowing when to stay quiet, how to mimic calm, and what to do so teachers would leave me alone.

Inside, though, I was still that restless, inquisitive, passionate kid who wanted more:

- *More adventure*

- *More learning*

- *More freedom*

The traits I was once punished for—

my energy, my curiosity, my intensity—

are the same ones that shape me today.

But back then, I didn't know that.

I only knew I felt out of sync.

Drawn to the extraordinary. Obsessed with big stories and even bigger questions.

I knew I wasn't built for quiet.

I just didn't know how to live loud—yet.

. . .

The world wasn't ready for me.

And in truth, I wasn't ready for the world, either.

Not yet.

But kids like me—the ones labeled *"too much"*?

We're not too much at all.

We're just built for more.

Chapter 2

CHASING DOPAMINE ACROSS THE WORLD

WHY I TRAVELED NONSTOP, YET NEVER FELT SETTLED

Some people are drawn to stability.

I was drawn to motion.

From the moment I could make my own decisions, I craved adventure, change, and the thrill of the unknown.

Routine felt like suffocation.

Predictability was my worst nightmare.

So, I traveled. A lot.

From Poland to Australia.

From England to Argentina.

From Italy to Israel.

I existed in a constant state of movement, forever chasing the next big experience, the next challenge, the next surge of excitement.

Each new place felt like a fresh start.

An opportunity to reinvent myself.

To learn something new.

To outrun boredom before it had the chance to catch me.

At the time, I thought I was simply adventurous.

Looking back now, I recognize the truth:

I was running on pure ADHD survival mode.

My brain craved novelty and thrived on the dopamine rush of:

- *New faces*

- *New languages*

- *New foods*

- *New possibilities*

I still remember stepping off the plane in Australia for the first time—

the humid air hitting my skin—

and feeling like my life had just cracked wide open.

Of course I'd try surfing.

Of course I'd explore the outback.

But stay put for more than a year?

Not a chance.

It took a while to understand why this constant motion appealed to me so deeply.

The ADHD brain is wired to seek novelty, excitement, and challenge—

things travel provides in abundance.

New environments kept my attention locked in the present.

Unpredictable days fueled the adrenaline that made me feel most alive.

Meeting new people gave me an endless supply of stories, personalities, and perspectives.

And without a daily routine, I was never forced to confront the monotony I loathed so deeply.

But the truth?

I wasn't just running toward adventure.

I was also running away.

• Away from boredom

• Away from expectations

• Away from the feeling of being trapped in a world that wanted me to sit still

I learned the hard way:

You can't outrun your own brain.

The restlessness and impulsivity followed me to every continent—

lingering long after the thrill of a new place had faded.

Dopamine highs never last forever.

Eventually, I realized...

I needed more than a plane ticket to keep my life from unraveling.

Travel taught me something crucial:

While newness fuels my spirit,

a certain amount of stability helps me thrive.

It's not that I needed to abandon my wanderlust or shut down my curiosity.

I just had to learn how to balance excitement with grounding—

to anchor myself when the rush wore off.

I began to wonder if the real challenge wasn't finding the next far-flung destination,

but rather learning how to stay.

How to be content in one place long enough to build something meaningful—

even if my brain itched for constant change.

As thrilling as it was to live perpetually on the move,

I started seeing that I couldn't run forever.

And so, with a well-worn passport and a heart still pounding from the rush of the unknown,

I found myself at a crossroads:

Keep chasing new places to avoid the challenges of *ordinary* life...

or discover how to create a life I didn't need to escape from.

The question was no longer where to go next—

but how to exist in one place without losing my spark.

Without losing myself.

It was a puzzle I wasn't sure how to solve just yet.

But one thing was clear:

Motion was no longer enough.

I would have to find a new way forward—

one that embraced my need for novelty,

yet offered me a sense of genuine grounding.

Because sometimes, the bravest journey

isn't crossing an ocean—

it's staying put and confronting what's inside you.

Chapter 3
HITTING THE WALL
WHEN THE WORLD STOPPED—BUT MY BRAIN DIDN'T

When COVID hit, the world went into slow motion—

but my ADHD brain didn't.

For years, I had thrived on chaos, speed, and unpredictability.

The fast-paced world of startups, international business development, raising money, making connections—

I was built for that.

The thrill of negotiations.

The jet-setting lifestyle.

The excitement of the unknown.

It was pure dopamine fuel for my ADHD mind.

And then, in an instant, everything stopped:

- *Travel ceased*

- *Face-to-face meetings vanished*

- *High-energy interactions disappeared almost overnight*

But it wasn't just the pandemic that forced me to slow down.

I had also become a single mother.

Raising a child alone, with no family support, while trying to navigate a world suddenly on pause...

it felt like being handed a new script I hadn't rehearsed for.

I couldn't pack my bags and hop to another country whenever restlessness set in.

My world shrank to a home, a laptop, and the relentless responsibility of being both parent and provider.

For the first time, I had to stay.

I couldn't run.

And that's when I realized just how much I had relied on constant motion to keep me afloat.

At first, I tried to power through.

Every morning, I'd open my laptop, stare at the sea of emails, Zoom meetings, and spreadsheets, and push myself to focus.

But something was off.

There was no thrill, no adrenaline, no fire to keep me going.

Everything that used to fuel me had vanished.

And my brain resisted the work like it was an electric fence.

Tasks I once loved turned into mental quicksand.

I wasn't just bored. I was disconnected.

Every day felt like wading through sludge, and I finally saw it for what it was:

Burnout—creeping up on me in real time.

That's when the question hit me like a freight train:

What if I stopped forcing myself into a career that no longer served me?

For so long, I had defined myself by my job—by the chaos and excitement it brought—

but now it felt suffocating.

If I wasn't that high-powered businessperson...

then who was I?

I realized I had spent years chasing success.

But it was time to start chasing *purpose*.

- *Writing*

- *Creativity*

- *Authenticity*

Those were the things that truly lit me up.

Yet stepping away from a career that "made sense" and into something uncertain?

Terrifying.

Still, a part of me knew:

I couldn't keep going the way I had.

It was time to stop merely surviving—

and start creating.

So I let go.

I released the career path that no longer matched who I was becoming—

and began channeling my energy into writing this book.

The moment I did?

I felt a spark of life again.

It was like finally giving my ADHD brain the novelty, creativity, and meaning it had been screaming for.

Because here's the truth:

ADHD isn't about failing to fit into the system.

It's about *creating a system that fits you.*

Chapter 4

THE ADHD BREAKTHROUGH

THE MOMENT EVERYTHING CLICKED

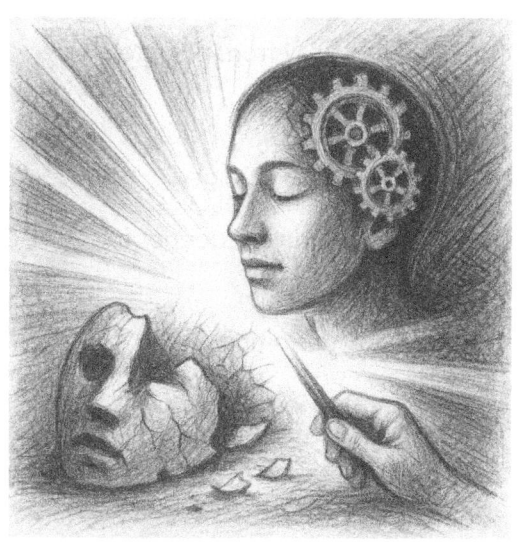

I used to think I was just bad at life.

Seriously.

I believed I lacked discipline.

That I was lazy.

That I couldn't stick with anything simply because I didn't try hard enough.

It seemed like everyone else moved through life with a built-in instruction manual,

while I was running purely on chaos—

always one deadline away from disaster.

Then, one day, everything changed.

It wasn't until I started diving deeper into ADHD research—

not the dry, textbook definitions,

but the real, lived experiences of ADHD brains like mine—

that I had my *holy sh*t* moment.

I caught myself thinking:

Wait a second... I'm not broken. My brain just works differently.

Suddenly, my entire life made sense:

• *The unfinished projects?* Executive dysfunction.

• *The random bursts of hyper-productivity followed by burnout?* Dopamine-driven motivation.

• *The overwhelm from simple tasks?* Task initiation paralysis.

• *That never-ending loop of procrastination, anxiety, and guilt?* ADHD perfectionism.

Once I recognized those patterns for what they were,

I knew I needed professional confirmation.

So I went for a proper assessment.

I remember sitting there, spilling my entire life story—

my struggles, my knack for hyper-focusing on random obsessions,

my tendency to completely ignore actual responsibilities.

The doctor smiled and said,

"You don't have to convince me—you're a textbook case."

Just like that, I wasn't crazy.

I wasn't lazy.

I wasn't broken.

I was ADHD.

With my diagnosis in hand, I threw myself into research mode.

(*Because if there's one thing ADHDers excel at, it's going down a rabbit hole when something really interests us.*)

I tested everything I could think of.

• *Adjusting my diet*

• *Incorporating more movement*

• *Managing my time in a way that made sense for my brain*

Medication? Yes, that helped.

But I also realized I needed lifestyle changes.

And maybe more than that—mindset changes.

I learned that therapy and reframing were just as crucial as any external tool.

Letting go of self-judgment?

It mattered more than I'd ever imagined.

Understanding my ADHD changed everything.

I stopped forcing myself into productivity systems designed for neurotypical minds.

Instead, I began building frameworks that worked *with* my brain, not against it.

For the first time, I wasn't just getting by—

I was thriving.

Because ADHD isn't some tragic flaw.

It's a different operating system.

You just have to learn how to use it.

In the process of rewriting my own story,

I started seeing all of Nathan's (my amazing son) struggles in a new light.

All the resistance I'd felt about ADHD—especially regarding Nathan and his school life—

now made total sense.

I realized I couldn't keep rejecting solutions out of fear.

If I could break free,

then so could he.

And that's where Nathan's story begins.

Chapter 5

THE ADHD PARENT
REBELLION

PARENTING, INDEPENDENCE & PERSONAL GROWTH

Two ADHD brains, one mission—

and a whole lot of chaos.

Let me paint you a picture:

Nathan bounding around the living room, reenacting an epic battle between imaginary warriors at full volume...

while I'm pacing in the kitchen, completely lost in a tangle of overanalyzing thoughts.

One moment, he's mid-sentence on the couch.

The next, he forgets what he was saying and starts spinning in circles because... well, why not?

Meanwhile, I'm trying to remember why I walked into the kitchen in the first place.

Welcome to ADHD parenting.

It's chaos.

It's beautiful.

It's exhausting.

And it's utterly ours.

Nathan was diagnosed with ADHD at age nine—

not because I thought something was "wrong,"

but because his teachers were adamant.

Every school meeting felt like a courtroom trial:

• *"Nathan is too disruptive. He can't sit still. He interrupts."*

• *"He forgets his homework."*

• *"He's a distraction to other students."*

It was exhausting.

I pushed back:

"He's a brilliant child. He's creative. He just learns differently."

But all they wanted was medication.

Something to keep him in line.

I refused.

I was deep into spirituality, into Human Design, and I believed Nathan's brain was perfect as it was.

Giving him a pill to "fix" him felt like a betrayal.

So, I tried everything else:

• *Diet changes*

• *More structure*

• *Creative learning*

• *Endless patience*

Still, as Nathan grew older, the battles with school intensified.

By sixth grade, the cracks became impossible to ignore.

He was slipping behind academically.

His frustration soared.

His self-esteem took hit after hit.

Secondary school loomed—stricter teachers, tougher subjects,

and even less tolerance for his energy and spontaneity.

I realized I couldn't afford to be stubborn forever.

After my own ADHD breakthrough,

I finally saw what Nathan had been struggling with all along.

I sat him down, explained ADHD, and gave him the choice.

The day he first tried medication, he came home beaming.

His teachers praised him.

He finished his homework.

He even—miraculously—organized his backpack.

It wasn't about changing who he was.

It was about unlocking what had always been there.

In the classroom, medication helped him:

- *Focus*

- *Listen*

- *Participate in a structure that had always made him feel trapped*

But outside of school?

That's where we let ADHD run free.

We learned to keep structure flexible—because rigid routines only led to frustration.

We realized that energy must be channeled, not suppressed.

Sports, humor, movement, and creativity fueled him in ways a strict schedule never could.

And we discovered that authenticity mattered most of all.

I'd spent years trying to contort myself into neurotypical expectations.

But true success came the moment I embraced my own ADHD—

and taught Nathan to do the same.

For the first time, I wasn't battling the world or battling Nathan.

I was helping build a life that truly worked for both of us.

My son and I became an ADHD dream team.

And honestly?

I wouldn't trade it for anything.

Chapter 6

FROM CHAOS TO CLARITY

HOW ADHD BECAME MY
GREATEST BLESSING, NOT MY
BURDEN

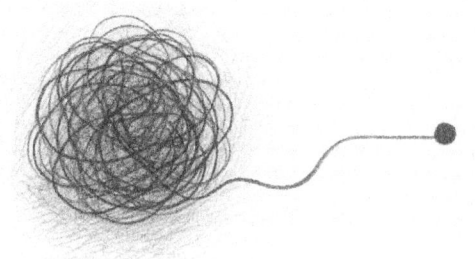

I used to view my ADHD as the villain of my life story—

the culprit behind every missed deadline, every restless night, every impulsive leap into the unknown.

But somewhere along the journey, I realized something radical:

ADHD isn't a curse.

It's my biggest, boldest asset.

THE ADHD HOME: A PLACE TO THRIVE

Nathan and I don't just share a living space.

We create one that suits our wiring.

If we want to dance in the kitchen at midnight, we do it.

If we're hyperfocused on an art project until 2 A.M., so be it.

When ADHD gets in our way, we call it the *venom*—

and name it so it loses its sting.

When it lights our creativity on fire, we call it our *superpower*.

We replaced the old shame and "should-haves" with acceptance, humor, and zero apology.

Somehow,

"You're too much" became

"We're exactly enough."

LESSONS & BLESSINGS

Don't let me sugarcoat it—

the path was messy.

I stumbled a thousand times.

Burned out.

Faced self-doubt daily.

But in that chaos, I discovered a core truth:

ADHD isn't something to fight.

It's an operating system that needs the right environment to shine.

Once I stopped wrestling my brain and started working with it,

the world opened up.

• *The same impulsivity that wrecked my finances?* Taught me resilience and adaptability.

• *The same restlessness that crashed me into walls?* Gave me unstoppable passion.

WHY "TOO MUCH" TURNED OUT TO BE PERFECT

So many people told me I was *"too much."*

Too loud. Too busy. Too inquisitive.

I believed them for years.

Tried to shrink myself into smaller boxes.

But the real pivot came when I realized:

"Too much" was the reason I succeeded.

• My *"excessive curiosity"* led me to explore half the globe.

• My *"inability to sit still"* kept me physically active, always chasing the next spark.

• My *"scattered thinking"* became a wellspring of creativity—in writing, parenting, problem-solving.

NATHAN: MY FAVORITE CO-PILOT

Raising Nathan revealed that I wasn't alone in this ADHD rollercoaster.

Seeing my energy and curiosity mirrored in him

made me love my own traits more.

The same restlessness that teachers complained about in him?

The same restlessness I'd always been scolded for?

Now I recognized it as unstoppable vitality—

a thirst for life that can't be contained.

We learned that success doesn't mean erasing ADHD quirks.

It means embracing them.

When we see each other's ADHD flare up, we laugh.

We pivot. We adapt.

We give each other permission to be weird, loud, and enthusiastic.

The *"too much"* label faded.

Because in our home,

"too much" is exactly right.

FINDING THE "CLARITY" IN THE CHAOS

It took a global pandemic.

A career upheaval.

A single-motherhood journey.

For me to finally get it:

ADHD wasn't my enemy.

It was the vehicle carrying me through every twist and turn.

Yes, the ride is bumpy.

Yes, I crash sometimes.

But the view out these ADHD windows?

It's spectacular.

- *I'm not lazy*—I'm unstoppable when something truly matters.

- *I'm not inconsistent*—I'm dynamic, seizing every spark.

- *I'm not flawed*—I'm wired for exploration, adventure, and expression.

A NOTE FOR EVERY ADHDER

If you've ever felt *"too big"* for the room, I see you.

If you've tried to fold yourself into smaller shapes just to fit, I feel you.

That shame, that guilt, that exhaustion from masking?

It doesn't have to be your story forever.

ADHD is a different operating system.

It's not about fixing yourself.

It's about creating environments that let you shine.

The moment you stop forcing yourself into *"normal"*

and start adapting your life to your brain?

That's when clarity emerges—

the kind that can launch you forward.

WRAPPING UP PART ONE: THE STORY THAT STARTED IT ALL

FROM SURVIVAL TO THRIVAL

YOU MADE IT THROUGH THE MESSIEST PART

Not because it was the hardest to read,

but because it was the closest to home.

Part One wasn't about theories.

It was about truth.

Real stories.

Raw moments.

The kind of lived chaos that doesn't show up in clinical definitions—

but definitely shows up in your laundry pile,

your Google calendar,

and your nervous system.

This wasn't just my story.

It was a mirror—

so you could start to see your own more clearly,

with compassion and without shame.

WHAT YOU JUST DID

You didn't read about ADHD like a diagnosis.

You lived through it like an identity.

You saw:

- The early signs you thought were just "bad habits"

- The spirals that were actually survival strategies

- The creativity inside your chaos

- The burnout behind your brilliance

You walked with me through:

- The fog

- The fire

- The meltdowns

- The miracles

And in doing that?

You stopped asking *"What's wrong with me?"*

And started asking,

"What's actually going on here?"

That shift?

It's massive.

Part 2

INSIDE THE ADHD BRAIN — THE SCIENCE BEHIND THE STORMS

HOW ADHD BRAINS REALLY WORK (AND WHY WE STRUGGLE). EACH CHAPTER BREAKS DOWN THE WIRING BEHIND YOUR WILD, WONDERFUL MIND.

BEFORE READING PART TWO: THE TRANSLATION YOU'VE BEEN WAITING FOR

DECODING YOUR ADHD OPERATING SYSTEM — NO PhD REQUIRED

NOW WE STOP GUESSING—AND START UNDERSTANDING

If Part One was the lived experience,

Part Two is the translation.

This isn't about planners, productivity hacks, or keeping your inbox at zero.

It's about the why.

Why your brain does what it does.

Why starting feels impossible but finishing can feel electric.

Why you care so deeply and crash just as hard.

Why focus isn't missing—it's just misunderstood.

THE ADHD TRUTH FILE

You're not lazy.

You're not broken.

You didn't invent this for TikTok.

ADHD is real.

It's genetic.

It's neurological.

It's not a trend.

It's a neurodevelopmental condition that affects how you regulate:

- Attention

- Time

- Emotion

- Motivation

- Energy

Here's what the science says:

- ADHD is about 76% heritable *(Faraone et al., 2005)*

- ADHD symptoms can shift with life stage, hormonal changes, and environment *(Turgay et al., 2011; Pataky et al., 2021)*.

- There are three core types: inattentive, hyperactive-impulsive, and combined *(APA, 2013)*

- It doesn't "go away"—it just changes shape *(Song et al., 2021)*

Here's what that might look like for you:

- You forget things that matter to you

- You freeze before simple tasks, then spiral with guilt

- You either sleep 3 hours or 13

- You feel everything—then shame yourself for being "too sensitive"

- You're incredibly focused... but only on the wrong thing, at the wrong time

- You plan everything. And start nothing

You're not flaky.

You're working with an operating system no one ever taught you how to navigate.

This next section?

It's here to help you do exactly that.

WHAT YOU'LL FIND IN PART TWO

Each chapter zooms in on a core ADHD challenge—

not to label it, but to explain what's actually happening underneath.

You'll learn:

- Why your brain craves novelty, urgency, and movement

- Why executive function short-circuits when you "should" be productive

- Why emotions explode fast, and linger longer than anyone sees

- Why time feels like fiction—until it's a five-alarm emergency

- Why sleep collapses, clutter multiplies, and shame loops

- Why your brain overlaps with anxiety, trauma, burnout, and more

- Why none of this means you're broken

And the best part?

Every chapter in Part Two connects to a matching chapter in Part Three.

So when something hits close to home?

Flip to the next section—

that's where the tools live.

HOW TO READ THIS SECTION (IF YOUR BRAIN IS TIRED)

- Start where it hurts—or where it helps

- Skip around. Follow your fire

- Reread the chapters that speak to your life

- Highlight the lines that hit

- Rest when it gets heavy. You're allowed

- You don't need to memorize. Just notice what lands

When something resonates?

Flip to Part Three.

That's where *"what now?"* becomes *"right here."*

THIS IS THE BRIDGE BETWEEN WHO YOU ARE AND WHAT YOU NEED

You've made it through the story part.

The memory part.

The emotional weather part.

Now, you're ready to understand the architecture underneath it all.

This isn't about fixing you.

It's about giving your brain the translation, the framework,

and the freedom it's always needed.

This is where the story meets the science.

And where the science becomes your strategy.

You're not just a person with ADHD.

You're a person with pattern, power, and potential—

and now?

You've got a map.

Let's go read it together.

Chapter 1

SO, WHAT IS ADHD, REALLY?

A DIFFERENT OPERATING
SYSTEM, NOT A BROKEN BRAIN

BRAIN BITE: THE TRUTH BENEATH THE TANGLE

Let's start with the elephant in the room:

ADHD is real.

It's not an excuse.

It's not *"just a kid thing."*

It's not caused by sugar, screen time, or some cosmic lack of willpower.

And it's definitely not a reflection of your intelligence, your effort, or your character.

ADHD is a neurodevelopmental condition, which means your brain was wired a little differently from the very beginning *(APA, 2013)*.

That wiring doesn't go away with age.

It affects how you focus, regulate emotions, manage time, remember things, and shift gears between tasks.

It's invisible on the outside—

but deeply felt on the inside.

Now picture your brain like a computer.

Most people run on the world's default operating system.

ADHD brains?

We're on custom firmware.

Faster in some places.

Glitchy in others.

Brilliant, unpredictable, beautifully chaotic—

and not always compatible with how society expects things to run.

And no, this metaphor isn't just cute—

it's backed by decades of research.

Neuropsychologists have redefined ADHD through the lens of executive function and brain network models *(Mahone & Denckla, 2017).*

That's where these metaphors come from—

they're not fluff.

They're science, translated into human.

Now imagine being handed a violin... but no one tells you you're left-handed.

You try to play like everyone else: awkward, frustrated, out of tune.

The problem isn't you.

It's that no one gave you the right setup.

That's what living with undiagnosed ADHD feels like.

Trying to perform on an instrument that has always felt a little off.

And when you finally realize it's not your fault?

That's when everything shifts.

Because here's the truth:

Your brain isn't broken.

It's just running a different operating system.

PERSONAL VIGNETTE: MY POST-EVAL "AHORA ENTIENDO"

I slid out of the neurologist's office feeling lightheaded.

The doctor had just confirmed what I had half-suspected all along: ADHD.

My eleven-year-old, hyperactive-impulsive whirlwind of a son, Nathan, had been diagnosed two years earlier.

Ever since, I'd been in detective mode—

binge-watching ADHD explainers on YouTube,

devouring audiobooks,

diving into neuroscience research,

scribbling frantic notes in the margins of every self-help book I could find.

I was trying to understand *his* world—long before I realized it was mine too.

On the drive home, I hit play on my flamenco playlist—

Spanish guitar, hand claps, the whole fiery mix.

I sang along, and suddenly, clarity hit harder than the rhythm.

"Ahora entiendo," I whispered to the rearview mirror.

"I know I have ADHD. I know Nathan has ADHD. And now I finally get why we do what we do."

The midnight Vespa obsession.

The bungee jump decision.

The research spirals.

Not random.

Not wrong.

Just data points on a map—leading me here.

That drive wasn't a commute.

It was a rebirth.

GENETICS: IT STARTS IN THE CODE

ADHD is highly heritable—about 76%, according to genetic studies *(Faraone et al., 2005)*.

If you have it, someone in your family tree probably does too.

Maybe your dad's wild stories suddenly make more sense.

Or your aunt's messy brilliance.

You didn't choose this brain.

You inherited it.

That's not a flaw.

That's a legacy.

And no—

it's not caused by bad parenting or too much screen time.

You didn't "become" this way.

You were born this way.

THE POWER OF NAMING: WHY LANGUAGE MATTERS

ADHD has existed longer than the acronym.

Back in 1968, it was called *Hyperkinetic Reaction of Childhood*.

Translation: *"Your kid is wild."*

Over time, the name shifted: ADD, then ADHD, and now?

We have three core presentations: inattentive, hyperactive-impulsive, and combined *(APA, 2013)*.

Why does it matter?

Because what we name, we shape.

And what we misname, we mistreat.

The language of ADHD has left so many people behind—

especially women, nonbinary folks, and people of color.

They were misdiagnosed, dismissed, or never seen at all.

Only now are we starting to see the full spectrum.

GROWN-UPS DON'T "OUTGROW IT"

Another myth:

ADHD is something you "grow out of."

Not true.

Recent studies show that 2.58% of adults still meet diagnostic criteria for persistent ADHD *(Song et al., 2021)*.

That's not mild. That's lifelong.

But it *looks* different with age.

Instead of blurting out in class, you might:

• Forget your groceries

• Miss a deadline

• Cry over a vague text message

The hyperactivity?

It doesn't disappear.

It turns inward—into anxiety, overthinking, shame, and burnout.

You didn't grow out of ADHD.

You got better at masking it.

FOCUS ISN'T BROKEN. IT'S UNPREDICTABLE.

Let's talk about the name:

Attention-deficit hyperactivity disorder.

Sounds like we *can't* focus, right?

But here's the truth:

We don't have a deficit of attention.

We have a dysregulation of it.

Too little when we need it.

Too much when we don't.

Rarely where we want it.

ADHD is a regulation disorder *(Barkley, 1997)*.

That means our brain struggles with:

- *Starting and stopping tasks*

- *Delaying gratification*

- *Redirecting attention*

- *Managing emotion and motivation*

- *Using working memory to plan ahead*

You know what you need to do.

But your brain doesn't always let you.

Especially when it matters most.

HYPERFOCUS: THE BEAUTIFUL TRAP

Here's the twist:

People with ADHD often have *laser-sharp* focus—

but only on certain things.

This is called hyperfocus.

And it's real.

During hyperfocus, dopamine flows, time disappears, the world fades.

You enter a tunnel of total engagement.

You might write a novel in a weekend...

or forget to eat, sleep, or call someone back *(Ashinoff & Abu-Akel, 2021)*.

Hyperfocus isn't the opposite of distraction.

It's the *flip side* of the same coin.

We don't have broken focus.

We have *all-or-nothing* focus.

YOUR ADHD IS STILL THERE—IT'S JUST CHANGED FORM

Symptoms don't vanish with age.

They evolve.

That hyper kid becomes the overwhelmed adult.

The daydreamer becomes the multitasker.

The big feelings become deep shame.

The prefrontal cortex—the part of your brain that plans, prioritizes, and pivots—develops more slowly in ADHD brains and matures later than in neurotypical development *(Arnsten, 2009)*.

So what looks like immaturity isn't immaturity.

It's developmental lag.

And once you're an adult?

You're expected to function.

To manage time.

To remember birthdays.

To be calm, collected, consistent.

But you're still wired the same way.

That's not failure.

That's reality.

THE ADHD OPERATING SYSTEM

So... what is ADHD, really?

It's not a broken brain.

It's a different *operating system*.

It's built for:

• *Rapid scanning*

• *Deep emotion*

• *Bold action*

• *Fast pivots*

• *Intense bursts of insight*

It craves movement, novelty, urgency, connection.

It stumbles with routine, monotony, stillness.

If you've felt like you never fit...

If you've sprinted through life, then collapsed in shame...

If you've blamed yourself for not thriving in a system that never fit you—

Let me say this clearly:

You're not lazy.

You're not broken.

You're not too much.

You're running a different system.

And now that you *know* that—

you can stop fighting it...

and start learning how to work with it.

WHERE DO WE GO FROM HERE?

Core Insight:

ADHD isn't broken. It's just different.

What now → Flip to Part 3, Chapter 1 for:

• *The Strengths & Struggles Map – your grown-up napkin blueprint*

• *Your OS, Not Their Planner – routines that honor your rhythm*

• *The Dopamine Compass – track what lights you up (or shuts you down)*

• *The "Not Broken, Just Different" Script Set – rewrite the shame script*

• *The ADHD OS Visualizer – a doodle-based view of your executive system*

You don't need more pressure.

You need tools that speak your language.

Chapter 2
THE MANY FLAVORS
OF ADHD

SPOILER: THERE'S MORE THAN
ONE RECIPE

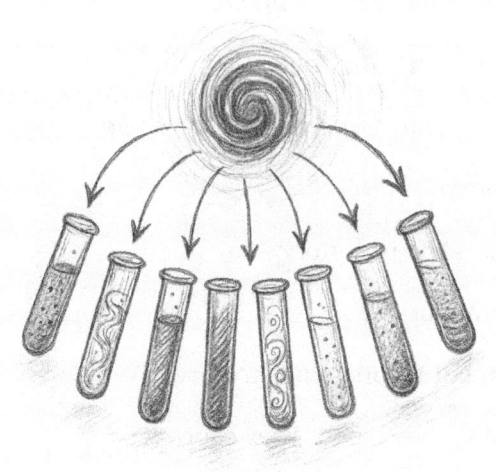

BRAIN BITE: UNDERSTANDING THE SPECTRUM

Let us clear something up right away:

ADHD is not one flavor.

It is a whole menu.

It does not look the same for everyone—

and it does not even look the same for you year to year.

Technically, the DSM-5 (yes, the big diagnostic manual) lists three official presentations *(American Psychiatric Association, 2013):*

• *Predominantly Inattentive*

• *Predominantly Hyperactive-Impulsive*

• *Combined*

But here is the real story:

Those categories?

They are not set in stone.

They shift. They blend. They evolve.

Your brain is responding to a moving target—life.

And life brings stress, hormones, sleep deprivation, new jobs, parenting, grief, joy, burnout... all of it.

The version of ADHD you are living with today might look totally different from how it showed up in high school—

or how it will look five years from now.

That is not inconsistency.

That is your brain adapting.

So if you have ever thought:

"Wait, I didn't used to struggle with this," or

"Why is this getting harder lately?"

You are not imagining it.

You are just seeing how dynamic your wiring actually is.

ADHD does not stay in its lane.

And neither do we.

PERSONAL VIGNETTE: THE COMBINED ROLLER COASTER

It was a Tuesday evening, and of course, I was late—again.

I laid on the horn at a Prius crawling through a green light.

"*¡Puta madre!*" I shouted, before switching to perfect Italian: *"Porca miseria!"*

My foot drummed on the brake pedal.

My shoulders tensed.

My heart pounded like it wanted to punch a hole in my chest.

How can people just sit there, motionless, when there is a world to conquer at warp speed?

Moments later, my hyperdrive stalled like a deflated balloon.

I pulled into the grocery store, adrenaline still crackling in my veins—

and totally forgot why I had come.

Standing in the express lane with a half-blank list, my brain drifted:

Quantum physics podcast.

A poem I meant to write.

Neon pizza sign.

That's my Combined ADHD life in a nutshell.

One second: multilingual road rage.

The next: a dreamy writer romanticizing frozen lasagna.

I used to resent the push-pull.

Now? I embrace it.

When the world's slow lane suffocates me, I let my hyper side rev.

When my brain floats off, I journal or brainstorm something new.

That glitch?

It is my superpower—my ADHD OS working in perfect, unpredictable harmony.

Once you own your blend,

there is no dream too big or lane too slow.

ADHD ISN'T ONE FLAVOR — IT'S A FULL MENU

Predominantly Inattentive Presentation (ADHD-I)

This is the quiet kind. The under-the-radar kind.

The kind that gets mislabeled as:

• Shy

• Lazy

• Spacey

• Unmotivated

It does not come with chaos in the classroom or loud interruptions.

It comes with drifting. Zoning out mid-sentence.

Reading the same paragraph four times and still not knowing what it said.

It is:

• Forgetting appointments

• Clicking between ten open tabs

• Avoiding that form you swore you'd fill out

It is not apathy.

It is your attention acting like smoke—

slipping through your fingers, always drifting somewhere else.

It is subtle.

But it's everywhere.

And it can wreck your routines before anyone—including you—realizes what is happening.

Predominantly Hyperactive-Impulsive Presentation (ADHD-HI)

This is the full-throttle version. The engine that never shuts off.

The kid who climbs furniture and blurts out answers.

The adult who paces during phone calls, interrupts meetings, starts three projects by breakfast.

It gets diagnosed earlier—especially in boys—

because it is louder, bolder, and harder to miss.

But adults live with this version too.

It just wears a productivity mask.

You move fast. Think fast. Talk fast. Do fast.

And then... you crash.

On the outside, it looks like energy.

On the inside, it often feels like pressure—

like a motor inside you revving at full speed

while the rest of the world moves in slow motion.

. . .

Combined Presentation (ADHD-C)

This is the hybrid model. The buffet brain.

You've got inattention and hyperactivity.

Some days, you're staring at a blinking cursor.

Other days, you've said yes to three things and missed them all.

You ghost people.

You triple-book yourself.

You're bored and overstimulated.

Wired and wiped.

It can feel like running two operating systems at once —both fighting for control.

But when you learn to channel it?

You can pivot fast. Think on your feet. Thrive in chaos.

This blend can be your superpower—

if you learn to ride the wave instead of getting dragged under it.

Sluggish Cognitive Tempo (SCT): The Overlooked Cousin

This one's not even in the DSM—yet.

But the research is growing *(Creque & Willcutt, 2021)*.

And if you live it? You know it's real.

SCT feels like walking through fog.

It is not hyper. It is not loud.

It is:

• Staring into space

• Losing your train of thought

• Moving through life like your brain is buffering

It's often misread as:

• Depression

• Laziness

• Disinterest

But it's not.

It's a different tempo.

A quieter kind of chaos.

When that tempo doesn't match school or work expectations?

You don't just feel slow—

you start to feel broken.

But you're not.

You've just been misunderstood.

. . .

Gender & Masking: The Hidden Struggles

ADHD doesn't discriminate.

But diagnostic systems? They do.

Girls, women, and nonbinary folks often present with quieter traits.

Inattentiveness. Overthinking. Overcompensating.

And they mask.

They try harder. Stay quieter. Overachieve. People-please.

They grow up being told to:

• Sit still

• Stop crying

• Be better

So they adapt.

Until they burn out.

One study found that long-term masking

increases the risk of anxiety and depression later in life *(Biederman et al., 2010)*.

But here's the thing:

You can't treat what you can't see.

And when ADHD hides behind perfectionism, politeness, or emotional armor?

It often gets missed until adulthood—

when the cost of hiding finally breaks the system.

YOU DESERVE THE RIGHT DIAGNOSIS

Maybe you see yourself in one of these profiles.

Maybe in all of them.

Maybe in different ones at different points in your life.

That's the point.

ADHD is not a box.

It is a spectrum—

with seasons, shifts, and phases.

Understanding how your ADHD shows up doesn't limit you.

It frees you.

It gives you language.

A map.

A way to stop blaming yourself—

and start working with your brain instead of against it.

Because once you know your pattern?

You can build the toolkit to match.

WHERE DO WE GO FROM HERE?

Core Insight:

Your ADHD has moods—

and it deserves matching tools.

What now → Flip to Part Three, Chapter 2 for:

• *Flavor-Check Diaries – name what version of you showed up today*

• *Tempo-Matching Strategy – match your tools to your brain speed*

• *Masking Awareness Log – track where you hide and where you are real*

• *Sensory Environment Tuner – design a world that doesn't overstimulate you*

• *Flavor-Specific Mini-Plans – one-pagers for each flavor of ADHD*

You are not inconsistent.

You are dynamic.

Build tools that flex with you.

Chapter 3

INSIDE THE ADHD BRAIN

NEUROCHEMISTRY & NETWORK DRAMA

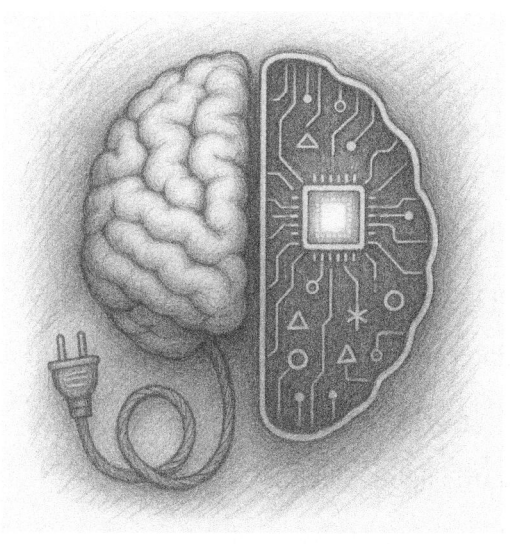

BRAIN BITE: A COFFEE CHAT ON ADHD NEUROBIOLOGY

Imagine your brain as a city during rush hour.

The lights are flashing.

Horns are blaring.

People are crossing against the signal.

And somewhere—somehow—there's a fire truck trying to make it through.

Now picture that city running on an outdated traffic system.

Messages—thoughts, emotions, decisions—are all trying to get where they're going via chemical messengers called neurotransmitters.

When those systems run smoothly?

You feel focused. Grounded.

Like things are (mostly) under control.

But in an ADHD brain?

• The traffic lights glitch

• Dopamine doesn't flow on schedule

• Noradrenaline bursts in and crashes out

• The control towers—planning, memory, emotional regulation—they show up late or not at all

You are not imagining the chaos.

It is not a character flaw.

It is your wiring.

And yeah... it's a lot.

This chapter isn't a lecture.

You don't need another textbook.

This is your behind-the-scenes tour.

A walkthrough of the messy, fascinating, infuriating world of ADHD neurobiology.

We're going to meet the major players in your brain's drama:

• The chemicals

• The networks

• The timing glitches

• The reasons everyday life feels like a high-stakes juggling act on a tightrope over lava

PERSONAL VIGNETTE: THE DOPAMINE WILD WEST

"Ciao, Principessa!" — The Midnight Vespa

It's 11:47 PM.

I've sworn off screens for the night.

Yet here I am—half-watching an Italian rom-com.

Suddenly, sun-drenched Amalfi Coast.

Heroine flying down the road on a Vespa.

My ADHD brain lights up like fireworks.

I need a Vespa. Right now.

Ten minutes later, I'm deep into Italian import websites.

There she is: a white Primavera, fresh from Milan.

I drop a deposit before midnight.

By morning?

I own a scooter I've never ridden.

The roads? A disaster.

The license process? Bureaucratic chaos.

Principessa becomes a glorified garage ornament.

Classic ADHD move:

A dopamine spark becomes a full-blown purchase.

We don't just daydream.

We dive.

The Bungee Jump Break

Teenage me, folding brochures at a mall job.

Across the parking lot?

A bungee tower.

My brain whispers:

Stay bored? Or jump headfirst?

Fifteen minutes later, I'm airborne.

No hesitation. No plan. Just adrenaline.

Because for an ADHD brain, boredom isn't inconvenient.

It's *painful.*

So we chase any jolt that brings us back to life.

DOPAMINE: THE MOTIVATION MOLECULE

Ah, dopamine. The elusive unicorn of ADHD brains.

It's the chemical that fuels motivation, curiosity, and the thrill of starting something new—

or even just the will to get out of bed.

It's your brain's internal reward signal.

In neurotypical brains, dopamine hums like a reliable playlist in the background.

In ours? It's a scratched vinyl that only plays during emergencies or last-minute flights.

Volkow et al. (2009) found that ADHD brains show reduced dopamine transporter and receptor availability in key reward-processing areas like the striatum and nucleus accumbens—regions that govern goal-directed behavior, delayed gratification, and emotional regulation.

Translation:

Our dopamine system runs cool—like trying to stream 4K video on a phone stuck at 2%.

That's why:

• Planning ahead feels like chewing on mental cardboard

• New ideas hit like a drug—sparkly, thrilling, impossible to ignore

• Finishing one project? Hilarious. Starting five? Effortless

You're not flaky.

You're neurochemical.

You're chasing a reward signal your brain doesn't release predictably.

You're trying to feel something—something that helps you shift from thought to action.

And too often, your own reward system just... leaves you on read.

NORADRENALINE & CORTISOL: THE STRESS CO-PILOTS

Noradrenaline (aka norepinephrine) and cortisol are your brain's stress and alert chemicals.

In a balanced brain, they help you:

• Wake up

• Stay focused

• Navigate danger or deadlines

In ADHD brains?

The volume knobs are broken.

One vague email.

One *"Can we talk?"* message.

Boom—cortisol spikes, noradrenaline surges, and your system floods.

Normally, *norepinephrine supports attention* and alertness.

But under emotional stress or social threat?

It joins cortisol in hijacking your brain's calm center.

Your *prefrontal cortex*—the part responsible for logic, planning, and regulation—goes offline *(Arnsten, 2009)*.

You're not bad under pressure.

You're neurochemically short-circuited.

That's why:

• *Tiny things feel massive*

• *Ambiguity shuts you down*

• *Conflict scrambles your entire system*

The co-pilots are panicked.

And the cockpit lights just flickered out.

THE PREFRONTAL CORTEX (PFC): THE EXECUTIVE HUB

Think of the PFC as your air traffic control tower.

It manages:

- Planning

- Self-control

- Emotional regulation

- Decision-making

In ADHD brains?

That tower is either:

- Late

- Distracted

- Or doesn't show up at all

Studies show ADHD brains develop more slowly in this area—by about 2–3 years in children *(Shaw et al., 2007)*.

And even in adults, it tends to activate less efficiently, especially under pressure or boredom.

You're not disorganized.

You're running a complex executive control system on low power and patchy Wi-Fi.

And that's not a character flaw.

That's neurology.

The PFC is responsible for what psychologists call "executive functions"—your brain's high-level processes.

But when it *does* show up?

Magic.

We ideate.

We pivot.

We create.

The catch?

Your PFC is like a genius freelancer.

Ghosts you for weeks.

Then shows up at 3 a.m. with brilliance.

THE DEFAULT MODE NETWORK (DMN): THE WANDERING MIND

This is your brain's idle mode—your background narrator.

In most people, it quiets down during focus.

In ADHD brains?

It. Never. Shuts. Up.

Research shows hyperconnectivity in this network in ADHDers *(Castellanos & Proal, 2011).*

That means it stays active *even when you're trying to focus.*

That's why:

• You rehash old conversations

• You spiral on what-if fears

• You wonder what would happen if your plane exploded mid-air

Trying to read one email while your DMN throws a party?

It's like trying to study during a rave.

THE GUT-BRAIN CONNECTION

Here's the twist no one talks about:

Your gut isn't just about digestion.

It's part of your brain team.

Biologically.

About 90% of your serotonin—plus precursors to dopamine—are produced in your gut.

So if your gut is off (inflammation, imbalance, low diversity)?

Your brain suffers.

One study found ADHDers often have altered gut microbiomes, which may influence mood, attention, and inflammation *(Gkougka et al., 2022)*.

That's why:

• *Sleep, nutrition, and gut health are not "just wellness fluff"*

- *Kombucha might actually help your focus*

- *A balanced belly = better brain chemistry*

Yes, that probiotic yogurt might be doing more than you think.

SO, WHAT'S REALLY GOING ON?

ADHD isn't about broken focus.

It's about:

- *Neurochemical chaos*

- *Delayed signal timing*

- *Internal shutdowns*

- *Sensory overload*

- *Scrambled feedback loops*

Your brain:

- Runs low on dopamine

- Craves novelty and urgency

- Overreacts to stress

- Struggles to shift from thought to action

- Crashes after every high

You are not undisciplined.

You are not lazy.

You are running a high-powered, nonlinear,
unpredictable operating system

in a world built for linear, slow, controlled machines.

You don't need to be fixed.

You need to know your wiring—

and build a life that works with it.

WHERE DO WE GO FROM HERE?

Core Insight:

Motivation isn't magic.

It's chemistry.

What now → Flip to Part 3, Chapter 3 for:

• *The Dopamine-First Morning Flow – fuel your fire, not your to-do list*

• *Food as a Dopamine Pharmacy – eat for fuel, not shame*

• *The Gut-Brain Dopamine Tracker – listen to your belly before your planner*

• *Cortisol Reset Loops – calm your co-pilots*

• *Energy-Ramping Micro-Rituals – spark your system without pushing it*

• *Meds: A Personalized Approach – support your fire, don't suppress it*

You don't need to force focus.

You need to feed the fire.

Chapter 4

EXECUTIVE DYSFUNCTION

WHY STARTING IS HARDER THAN
FINISHING A NETFLIX SERIES

BRAIN BITE: NAVIGATING THE EXECUTIVE FUNCTION MAZE

If ADHD is a different operating system,

then executive dysfunction is what happens

when your brain's launch sequence glitches.

You know what to do.

You want to do it.

You've promised to do it.

And still... nothing.

You stare at the task.

You circle it.

You plan it.

You journal about it.

Maybe even color-code it.

But you do not launch.

Or you launch too late.

Or in the wrong direction—with no pants on.

This is not laziness.

It's not a motivation issue.

It's what happens when the systems responsible for:

• Planning

- Memory

- Activation

- Emotion regulation

- Time awareness

can't coordinate under pressure.

Executive function is like your brain's CEO—

tasked with managing decisions, shifting gears,

and regulating behavior under pressure.

In ADHD brains, that CEO is overwhelmed,

under-supported,

or sometimes just... out to lunch.

This isn't just forgetfulness.

It's a full-blown system crash—

one that shows up as shame, overwhelm, impulsivity, and burnout.

It's not a lack of willpower.

It's a neurological bottleneck.

PERSONAL VIGNETTE: PARALYSIS, PERFECTION & PASSPORT FIASCOS

The Paralyzing Pursuit of Perfection

Two years ago, I fell head-over-heels into Human Design.

Thirty-seven browser tabs open.

Flamenco guitar playing.

Hyperfocus blazing.

I mapped an entire book.

Courses. Workshops. Big vision stuff.

And then came that whisper:

"Am I even qualified?"

"What if someone else already nailed it?"

"Who do I think I am?"

My passion iced over into paralysis.

I shelved the whole thing.

Told myself I'd come back to it *"when I'm ready."*

Spoiler: *ready* never came.

Not until I got my ADHD diagnosis

and realized I'd been letting fear and perfectionism shut me down for years.

. . .

The Passport Fiasco

Flight booked.

Outfits planned.

Pinterest board filled with cafés I'd hit in Rome.

But renew my passport?

Nope.

It felt boring. Bureaucratic. Non-urgent.

Suddenly, it's the night before the flight—

and I'm in full crisis mode, racing to fill out forms,

find a 24-hour photo center,

and beg the universe—or a miracle employee—to save me.

These aren't just "oops" moments.

They're textbook executive dysfunction:

• Tasks that don't get done

• Until they explode

• Then spiral into chaos

It's not just procrastination.

It's a neural stutter that sounds like:

"I'll do it soon..."

Until soon becomes *oh no*.

TASK INITIATION: THE STUCK ENGINE

Starting a task with ADHD is not about willpower.

It's about neurology.

It's your brain sitting there—foot on the gas—engine revving...

but stuck in neutral.

You want to go.

You need to go.

But your ignition doesn't fire.

Studies show ADHDers experience sluggish activation in the brain's "go circuit"

—specifically in the dorsal anterior cingulate cortex and striatal pathways *(Weigard et al., 2019)*.

That means:

• *The spark to move?* Sometimes never comes.

• *So instead of starting?* We scroll. Reorganize. Re-watch the show we already watched.

• *Until panic or pressure slams the pedal.*

And we launch.

TIME BLINDNESS: THE MYTH OF "LATER"

Here's how time works in an ADHD brain:

There's *Now.*

And *Not Now.*

That's it.

Time isn't a straight line.

It's a fog bank.

You know something is due next week...

and still treat it like fiction.

You sort Google Drive folders

instead of prepping for tomorrow's meeting.

Until it is tomorrow.

And crisis-you takes the wheel.

Barkley (1997) called this *temporal myopia—*

short-sightedness about the future.

It's not that we don't care.

It's that the future doesn't feel real.

WORKING MEMORY WIPEOUTS

Working memory is your mental sticky note.

- "The tea is steeping."

- "You left the passport on the table."

- "You were in the middle of writing an email."

But with ADHD?

That sticky note slides off the mental fridge in seconds.

Research shows we struggle especially when juggling multiple steps *(Martinussen et al., 2005)*.

It's not laziness.

It's like trying to carry water in a colander.

PROCRASTINATION LOOPS & EMOTIONAL AVOIDANCE

Avoid the task.

Feel guilty.

Panic.

Sprint.

Crash.

Repeat.

It's not bad planning.

It's survival.

We don't avoid tasks because they're hard.

We avoid them because they're *loaded*.

Perfectionism.

Fear of failure.

Fear of judgment.

That one email?

It's not just a message.

It's a test of your worth, your identity, your capacity.

ADHDers toggle between "cool" cognitive systems and "hot" emotional systems *(Castellanos et al., 2006).*

When the emotional brain grabs the wheel?

That to-do list becomes a monster.

DECISION PARALYSIS AND THE VALUE GLITCH

You've got five options.

None of them feel quite right.

Your brain spins.

You over-research.

You stall.

Or you pick impulsively—then second-guess everything.

ADHD brains often have dysfunction in the orbitofrontal cortex—

the area that evaluates risk and reward *(Dekkers et al., 2021).*

That's why:

• Choosing between three jobs, two apartments, or even lunch...

can feel like a hostage negotiation.

Nothing feels safe.

So we shut down.

Not because we don't care.

But because nothing feels certain enough to risk.

DISORGANIZATION LOOPS

Clutter is not just visual.

It's *mental noise*.

Every sock on the floor.

Every tab left open.

Every list left half-finished.

And when your brain is juggling:

• Low working memory

• Time blindness

• No task ignition

...even cleaning the kitchen feels like moving a mountain.

Studies show ADHDers have reduced connectivity in the areas that manage task sequencing *(van Rooij et al., 2015)*.

That's why your kitchen is half-clean.

The suitcase is half-packed.

The taxes are half-started.

And your brain is muttering:

"Why am I like this?"

SO, WHAT'S REALLY GOING ON?

Executive dysfunction isn't about laziness.

It's what happens when your internal control panel short-circuits.

You're built for bursts of brilliance.

Not slow, step-by-step manuals.

Here's what's happening:

• *Poor ignition* → You want to start, but your brain says: Meh.

• *Disrupted internal clocks* → You blink, and it's tomorrow.

• *Short-term memory hiccups* → What were you doing again?

- *Emotional overdrive* → One comment = full shutdown.

- *Clutter overload* → Your outer chaos reflects your brain.

- *Decision glitches* → Every option feels wrong.

You're not broken.

You're high-voltage.

You're low-regulation.

And you're trying to survive in a world built for spreadsheets and steady pacing.

Once you see the pattern,

you can stop blaming yourself.

And start building a life that actually works.

WHERE DO WE GO FROM HERE?

Core Insight:

You are not lazy.

You're stuck.

And stuck has a workaround.

What now → Flip to Part 3, Chapter 4 for:

• *Two-Minute Launchers – micro-starts that bypass the freeze*

• *Time Blindness Visual Anchors – make time visible and gentle*

• *If-Then Rescue Scripts – lifelines when logic goes offline*

• *Memory Anchors – externalize the chaos in your head*

• *The Body-Double Blueprint – borrow ignition from someone else's steady presence*

Your brain doesn't need more pressure.

It needs co-regulation.

Visual cues.

And the tiniest spark to begin.

Chapter 5
HORMONES AND ADHD
YOUR SYMPTOMS HAVE CYCLES

BRAIN BITE: THE HORMONE-DRIVEN ADHD ROLLER COASTER

Here's something they don't tell you at diagnosis:

ADHD doesn't show up the same way every day.

Some days, you're on fire—

crossing things off, in the zone, like you hacked the system.

Then suddenly...

you're crying in your car because someone left you on read.

Or you can't remember how to reply to an email.

You're not unraveling.

You're riding hormones.

ADHD isn't a steady, predictable state.

It surges.

It dips.

It sharpens.

It crashes.

Sometimes it disappears, only to slam back in.

One week you're productive and upbeat.

The next?

You're rage-cleaning the kitchen at midnight or convinced your life is falling apart because you forgot a birthday.

That chaos isn't just emotional.

It's chemical.

Hormones like estrogen, testosterone, cortisol, and thyroid hormones don't just affect mood—

they directly shift how your ADHD brain functions.

And since ADHD already impacts regulation,

those shifts hit harder.

If you've ever asked:

"Why did this feel manageable last week and impossible today?"

You're not making it up.

You're feeling your internal chemistry in real time.

This chapter isn't a lecture.

It's a reality check—

a map to help you recognize when ADHD is shifting shape

because your hormones are shifting the rules.

PERSONAL VIGNETTE: THE CHOCOLATE RUN & THYROID CRASH

The Pre-Period Chocolate Run

It's Wednesday afternoon.

Nathan and I are watching *Coco* for the third time this month.

Halfway through *Remember Me*, I'm sobbing—

like I'm in the Land of the Dead looking for my family.

Nathan peeks over.

"Mom, are you okay?"

I nod, trying to explain that sometimes,

my emotions go up to eleven—especially the week before my period.

Estrogen drops.

Focus disappears.

Mood tanks.

Nathan, the empathy expert, sprints to the kitchen.

He returns with Raffaello chocolates and Haribo gummies.

Within minutes, the sugar—and more importantly, the understanding—

pulls me back from the edge.

It wasn't just sugar.

It was care.

He got it.

Even before I did.

The Stress-Fueled Thyroid Crash

But hormones don't just cycle monthly.

They also collapse under pressure.

My collapse came quietly:

Weight loss. No appetite. Sleep vanished. Brain on fire.

I was spinning, organizing drawers, skipping meals—

but ignoring the signs.

A good friend looked at me one day and said:

"Pati, people over 40 don't spontaneously lose weight. Go get checked."

Then he paused.

"Also... you kind of look like a little boy."

I laughed. Then I listened.

Diagnosis: hyperthyroidism.

Turns out, long-term cortisol overload can tip your immune system into overdrive (*Weetman, 2000*).

Mine did.

My immune system produced antibodies that attacked my thyroid—

a full-body betrayal I didn't see coming.

Those antibodies triggered the hormone flood (*Arnsten, 2009*):

metabolism, mood swings, thoughts, heart rate— everything went into overdrive.

It looked like ADHD.

Until it didn't.

Until it became a medical emergency hiding in plain sight.

So yes—ADHD and hormone chaos are linked.

But sometimes, the problem isn't ADHD at all.

Trust your body.

If something feels off, it probably is.

ESTROGEN & PROGESTERONE: THE CYCLE THAT SPINS THE BRAIN

If you menstruate and have ADHD, you've probably asked:

"Why am I totally functional one week and an emotional disaster the next?"

Here's why: your hormones are driving the bus.

Estrogen boosts dopamine.

It lights up your prefrontal cortex.

It upgrades your working memory.

When estrogen rises, symptoms like brain fog and disorganization often *ease*.

You feel clearer, more regulated.

Even *normal*.

Then comes the luteal phase.

Estrogen crashes.

Progesterone takes over.

Suddenly:

- You lose focus mid-sentence

- Little things make you cry or scream

- Rejection hits like a gut punch

- Motivation evaporates

• Teens may get a hyperactivity spike

This "double-whammy" effect—estrogen's rise followed by a crash—amplifies both impulsivity and emotional reactivity *(Eng et al., 2024).*

You're not losing your mind.

You're riding the drop.

TESTOSTERONE: RISK, REWARD, AND RESTLESSNESS

Testosterone also shapes ADHD symptoms— especially around risk, reward, and stimulation.

ADHD already craves dopamine.

Testosterone amplifies that.

In testosterone-dominant bodies, this often looks like:

• Physical hyperactivity

• Bold or risky impulsivity

• Quick, high-stakes decisions

• Behaviors that get flagged early in school

That's part of why boys tend to be diagnosed earlier.

But let's be clear:

Girls, women, and nonbinary folks feel it too.

They just internalize it more—

and get missed more.

THYROID CHAOS HIDING IN PLAIN SIGHT

Thyroid hormones impact:

• Focus

• Energy

• Mood

• Memory

Sound familiar?

Even subtle thyroid dysfunction can mimic ADHD symptoms *(Zhu et al., 2006).*

It flares most during hormonal transitions:

Puberty. Pregnancy. Perimenopause.

And often?

It's brushed off.

Labeled as anxiety.

Or burnout.

Or *"just hormones."*

This is why ADHDers—especially women—need their thyroid checked regularly.

Because sometimes, what looks like executive dysfunction

is actually a thyroid screaming for help.

IT'S NOT YOU — IT'S THE CHEMISTRY STORM

Hormones aren't a footnote.

They're a full system-wide variable.

They reshape:

• How you think

• How you feel

• How ADHD shows up in your life

If your ADHD feels different each season, each week, each *day*—

you're not unstable.

You're chemically shifting.

And if you're tracking it?

That's not "extra."

That's survival.

THE BIG TRANSITIONS: PUBERTY, PREGNANCY, PERIMENOPAUSE

Hormones spike and crash hard during these transitions.

And each phase reshapes your ADHD.

Puberty? Total chaos.

Pregnancy? Clear-headed focus.

Postpartum? Numbness, then crash.

Perimenopause? I'm not there yet—

but you better believe I'll be prepared when it comes.

These shifts aren't random—they're backed by research that maps how ADHD symptoms change across the hormonal lifespan (Young et al., 2020).

I journaled through each season.

Mapped what worked. What failed. What saved me.

This became my compass.

You can make one, too.

THE ADHD + HORMONES EQUATION

ADHD doesn't live in isolation.

It lives in a *body*—

a hormone-driven, ever-changing body.

Hormones are not background noise.

They are *messengers*.

They influence:

• Attention

• Motivation

• Memory

• Mood

• Focus

And when they shift?

ADHD symptoms do too.

Sometimes they get louder.

Sometimes they vanish.

Sometimes they show up in disguise.

That's why:

• Tracking your cycle isn't "extra"

• Getting your thyroid checked isn't a side quest

• Managing cortisol isn't just for wellness influencers

This isn't "nice to have."

It's maintenance for your operating system.

Patrycja Marta Jerushalmy

If ADHD is how your brain runs,

then hormones are the weather.

You don't have to control the storm.

You just have to learn how to sail through it.

WHERE DO WE GO FROM HERE?

Core Insight:

You're not overreacting.

You're cycling.

What now → Flip to Part 3, Chapter 5 for:

• *Cycle-Aware Symptom Tracker – map the tides of your energy*

• *Follicular vs. Luteal Phase Planning – align your schedule to your cycle*

• *Thyroid Symptom Advocacy Script – speak your body's language*

• *Cortisol Recovery Ritual – reset when stress hijacks your system*

• *Hormonal Transition Map – navigate puberty, pregnancy, and perimenopause*

You don't have to push through the crash.

You can ride the wave.

Chapter 6

EMOTIONAL & SENSORY DYSREGULATION

FEEL ALL THE FEELS—FAST
AND LOUD

BRAIN BITE: WHY YOUR EMOTIONS HIT LIKE THUNDERCLAPS

Let's set the record straight—ADHD isn't just about attention.

It's about regulation.

And that includes your focus, your energy, your impulses...

and your emotions.

So if you've ever:

• Gone from *"I'm fine"* to *"I'm melting down"* in 0.7 seconds

• Teared up from a tone of voice

• Felt gutted by a passing glance

• Wanted to rip off a shirt tag in public

• Felt like someone brushing against you was an attack on your soul

That's not you being "too sensitive."

That's your nervous system doing what it's wired to do:

Respond. Loudly. Instantly. Fully.

You're not imagining the intensity.

You're feeling it—because your brain is built to feel it.

ADHD doesn't just affect how you think.

It affects how deeply—and how quickly—you feel.

This isn't a flaw.

It's real.

And once you name it, you can stop blaming yourself for the thunderclaps.

PERSONAL VIGNETTE: THE WEIGHT OF REJECTION & THE PERFECTION TRAP

I don't remember much from being four.

Except that my mom's face was my emotional North Star.

I was her whole world—until my baby brother arrived.

Suddenly, I was *"a big girl now."*

No more tears.

My safe place vanished.

Every misstep brought disapproval.

Every loud cry, a side-eye.

That shame?

It has a name: *Rejection Sensitive Dysphoria (RSD).*

It's not just *"taking things personally."*

It's feeling rejection—real or imagined—so intensely it burns.

• A single B on a test? → Failure

• A sarcastic joke? → Proof you're a burden

• A glance? → A dagger

My response?

Perfectionist chameleon mode.

I shape-shifted to fit every expectation.

Grades. Hobbies. Even my personality.

I masked constantly.

I performed "fine" even when I wasn't.

And every success came with a whisper:

"*What if this isn't enough?*"

So I raised the bar.

Fell harder.

Then did it all again.

I still feel it.

I can nail a presentation, feel untouchable...

and spiral from one offhand comment.

But here's the truth:

My sensitivity isn't my downfall.

It's my superpower.

I care fiercely.

I feel deeply.

Yes, I cry easily.

And all of that—

the fire, the empathy, the cost of masking—

brought me here.

Not to fix it.

But to finally write about it.

Because "too much" emotion?

Isn't too much.

It's just human.

THE BRAIN BEHIND THE OUTBURST

Emotions aren't random.

They're circuits.

In ADHD brains, the amygdala—our emotional threat detector—runs hot.

And the prefrontal cortex—our rational brake pedal— often lags behind.

This is not a character flaw.

It's a neurological delay *(Shaw et al., 2014)*.

You accelerate instantly.

But your brakes?

They sputter. Or fail.

That's not immaturity.

It's neurophysiology.

Sometimes we shut down.

Sometimes we explode before we know what hit us.

REJECTION SENSITIVITY: THE PAIN OF A RAISED EYEBROW

RSD isn't in the DSM, but nearly every ADHDer will tell you:

It's real.

It's the shame spiral when:

- Someone doesn't text back

- A friend seems "off"

- A coworker changes their tone

Suddenly your brain rewrites the whole relationship—

and blames you.

One study found kids and teens with ADHD often interpret neutral feedback as deeply personal *(Bondü & Esser, 2015).*

Adults feel it too—

but we've had more time to internalize the shame.

This isn't emotional fragility.

It's a nervous system treating rejection like danger.

And setting off all the alarms.

PERFECTIONISM AND THE SHAME LOOP

Here's the paradox:

We struggle to finish things...

yet hold ourselves to impossible standards.

Why?

Because failure doesn't just sting.

It *defines us*—if we let it.

Research links ADHD perfectionism to emotional impulsiveness—especially the kind that turns small mistakes into panic spirals *(Barkley & Fischer, 2010)*.

It doesn't just flag errors.

It panics about them.

So we:

• Over-function

• Overcompensate

• Mask

• Burn out

The loop is real:

Miss a task → feel like a failure → raise the bar → freeze → miss again → spiral deeper.

You're not failing.

You're just carrying ten internal alarms while running a marathon.

And still expecting a gold medal.

SENSORY OVERLOAD: WHEN THE WORLD'S TOO LOUD

You're in a café.

Someone's chair scrapes.

A baby screams.

The lights flicker.

Suddenly, your body wants to shut down.

This isn't "overreacting."

It's sensory dysregulation.

According to Polyvagal Theory, the vagus nerve helps regulate what stimuli gets filtered *(Porges, 2007)*.

In ADHD, that filter underfunctions.

So everything floods in.

That's why:

• You flinch at noises others don't notice

• You shut down in bright, crowded spaces

• The seam in your sock ruins your entire morning

• A chaotic room makes your skin crawl

This isn't hypersensitivity.

It's a nervous system struggling to regulate input.

. . .

MASKING EXHAUSTION: THE BURNOUT NO ONE SEES

Masking is when you hide the ADHD parts that feel like *"too much."*

You over-prepare.

You over-function.

You smile while you're spiraling.

And it works...

until it doesn't.

You get praised.

But you're exhausted.

Because you're burning extra energy just to appear "okay."

Research shows that many ADHD adults experience more functional impairment than it looks like from the outside *(Faraone et al., 2000).*

Eventually, the mask cracks.

You crash.

You blame yourself.

And you start over.

Again.

Masking isn't failure.

It's a survival tactic.

But no one can run on emergency mode forever.

THE EMOTIONAL SIDE OF ADHD IS NOT SECONDARY

This is where most professionals still get it wrong.

Emotional and sensory dysregulation aren't *side effects*.

They're *core wiring*.

The same networks that handle:

• Attention

• Planning

• Focus

Also handle:

• Emotion

• Impulse control

• Sensory regulation

When one part lags, the others do too.

That's why:

• Planners don't fix everything

• Productivity hacks collapse under stress

- "Just breathe" doesn't work when you're drowning

You can't build structure on a nervous system stuck in survival.

Before we talk strategy,

we talk regulation.

Not the polished kind.

The real, messy, daily kind.

You don't need to toughen up.

You need tools that meet your brain where it actually *is*.

Dear Little Me

WHERE DO WE GO FROM HERE?

Core Insight:

You feel deeply—

not because you're broken,

but because you're beautifully tuned in.

What now → Flip to Part 3, Chapter 6 for:

• *DBT-Style Emotion Riding – surf urges, name the storm, choose action*

• *Sensory Kit Builder – build your safety stash*

• *Sensory Safe Zones Map – design calm corners that calm your body*

• *Masking Fatigue Tracker – spot when you disappear to "pass"*

• *RSD Reality-Check Journal – rewrite the rejection narrative*

Your sensitivity is not your flaw.

It's your signal.

Chapter 7

ADHD IN REAL LIFE

WHEN THEORY MEETS YOUR
MESSY KITCHEN

BRAIN BITE: THE EVERYDAY EARTHQUAKE

It's one thing to understand dopamine on paper.

It's another thing to explain why your sink is full of dishes,

your phone bill is unpaid,

and you're crying in the shower

because someone texted back "K."

This is the part no one talks about enough:

ADHD doesn't just live in your brain.

It lives in your calendar.

Your bank account.

Your relationships.

Your clutter.

Your spirals.

Your patterns.

It leaks into everything.

Quietly. Loudly. All at once.

It doesn't look clinical.

It looks careless.

It looks selfish.

It looks like you're flaky, lazy, or arrogant.

But underneath?

It's not about being careless.

It's *regulation failure*.

It's *coping mechanisms that look like character flaws*.

It's a brain trying to survive in a world that was never designed for it.

This chapter isn't about symptoms.

It's about *impact*.

Let's walk through it.

No shame.

No sugarcoating.

Just the real stuff—the lived chaos of ADHD.

PERSONAL VIGNETTE: THE "YES" VACATION AND SOCIAL WIPEOUTS

The Retreat Fiasco

I used to think saying *"yes"* was my superpower—

until it became a wrecking ball.

A friend invited me to a beach retreat in Thailand.

Sun. Stillness. Deep workshops.

It was everything I thought I needed.

And I said yes—because that's what I do.

By day two:

• Dawn yoga wrecked my joints

• Silent meditations made me want to scream

• Artisanal tea tastings asked me to *sit still and savor* (lol)

My mind buzzed:

"I need change. I need fire. I live at 100 mph."

But I smiled.

Nodded.

Played along.

By day four?

My ADHD OS was fried.

I missed my chaos.

The Friendship Derail

Later that year, a friend told me her startup idea.

I interrupted:

"Oh! I had that exact idea while reorganizing my recycling!"

She blinked.

Paused.

I'd just hijacked her elevator pitch.

Then I ghosted her.

Not because I didn't care—

but because my brain had already sprinted off

to five new obsessions.

This is what ADHD looks like:

• Pleasing too much

• Buying too fast

• Ghosting people you love

• Being present... until you're not

But here's the truth:

Once you name these patterns,

you can start building bridges.

Saying *"no"* kindly.

Setting boundaries.

Creating one-touch systems that slow the spiral

before it starts.

FINANCIAL IMPULSIVITY: MUST-HAVE-IT-NOW SYNDROME

You walk into a store.

You're tired. Flat. Overstimulated.

Then you see it: the headphones. The sneakers. The Vespa.

Your brain says: *This will fix it.*

So you swipe.

Dopamine hits.

You feel alive...

for 30 minutes.

Then regret.

ADHD brains run low on *tonic dopamine*—the background fuel.

But we're hypersensitive to *phasic dopamine*—the spike from novelty *(Del Campo et al., 2011).*

That's why:

• Impulse buys feel like rescue missions

• Long-term goals feel fictional

• Budgeting feels fake

This isn't irresponsibility.

It's *neurochemistry.*

. . .

SOCIAL HICCUPS: INTERRUPTING, GHOSTING, BUFFERING

ADHD doesn't just mess with attention.

It messes with connection.

One study found ADHD brains struggle with social timing, emotional cues, and anticipating reactions *(Capuozzo et al., 2024).*

That's why we:

- Overshare

- Interrupt

- Ghost

- Over-apologize

- Then ghost again

Not because we don't care.

But because our relational software is glitchy—

and the world expects perfect real-time response.

You're not a bad friend.

You're just trying to connect with frayed executive wiring.

And it's exhausting.

. . .

EXECUTIVE DYSFUNCTION = CHRONIC CLUTTER

Your desk is a graveyard of unopened envelopes.

Your car is a rolling junk drawer.

You have five notebooks... and can't find one.

This isn't about cleanliness.

It's about *mental noise*.

Research shows ADHDers struggle to:

• Filter distractions

• Hold steps in mind

• Transition between tasks

• Maintain daily systems *(Willcutt et al., 2005)*

Clutter isn't a character flaw.

It's the fallout of cognitive fatigue.

You're not battling mess.

You're *living inside it*.

SELF-ESTEEM DIPS & IMPOSTER SYNDROME SPIRALS

Even when you succeed, a voice whispers:

"They don't know the truth."

"You got lucky."

"One mistake and you'll be exposed."

That's not insecurity.

That's trauma.

Years of masking, perfectionism, and emotional chaos

build *reflexive shame*.

Research shows this volatility is hardwired *(Shaw et al., 2014)*.

We minimize wins.

We magnify flaws.

Because no one sees the effort behind our output.

But it's real.

You're real.

And you've earned every inch of ground you stand on.

PEOPLE-PLEASING & OVERCOMPENSATION

You say yes too fast.

Volunteer too much.

Offer help before people ask.

Why?

Because ADHDers often over-function to feel safe.

To earn our spot.

To prevent rejection before it happens.

It's self-protection.

Until it becomes self-erasure.

What starts as kindness becomes performance.

You smile while shrinking.

Many of us were raised where love felt earned—through helpfulness, perfection, or being "easy."

It wasn't safe to need. So we over-functioned instead.

Research links this to rejection sensitivity and unrecognized trauma *(Surman et al., 2013)*.

You're not weak.

You've been compensating for a world that never made room for your wiring.

You're not selfish for saying no.

You're just done abandoning yourself.

BURNOUT CYCLES

ADHD doesn't come with a pause button.

It comes with:

Hyperfocus → Crash → Panic → Repeat.

We go all in.

Forget to eat.

Forget to sleep.

Then collapse.

Then feel guilty for crashing.

So we scramble to "catch up."

And do it again.

Studies show adults with ADHD report heightened stress and show variable cortisol recovery, especially by subtype *(Corominas-Roso et al., 2015)*.

That means:

- Recovery is slower

- Crashes last longer

- We burn out harder

This isn't bad planning.

It's a system running on fumes.

THE ADHD-SOCIETY GAP

ADHD doesn't live in isolation.

It lives in *context*.

And not everyone gets the same one.

Kids from low-income backgrounds are nearly *twice* as likely to develop ADHD—

and far *less* likely to be diagnosed or supported *(Russell et al., 2016).*

Why?

• Poverty adds pressure

• Pressure amplifies symptoms

• Bias delays care

And that gap?

It grows in adulthood:

• Job access

• Medical treatment

• Academic accommodations

• Cultural understanding

ADHD isn't an equal-opportunity disruptor.

Support shapes trajectory.

Naming this isn't divisive.

It's honest.

And honesty is where change begins.

REAL LIFE, REAL ADHD

This chapter isn't about shame.

It's about clarity.

- *Impulsive spending?* → Dopamine regulation

- *Missed texts?* → Social cognition

- *Shutdowns?* → Cortisol

- *Clutter?* → Executive fatigue

- *Perfectionism?* → Self-protection

- *Burnout?* → Nervous system exhaustion

You are not broken.

You're navigating a high-friction world

with a high-voltage brain—

and no one gave you the manual.

Until now.

WHERE DO WE GO FROM HERE?

Core Insight:

Function doesn't live in theory.

It lives in the fridge.

In your phone.

In your reality.

What now → Flip to Part 3, Chapter 7 for:

• *Impulse Pause Protocol – stop the scroll, the spend, the snap*

• *One-Touch Rule – clutter control that respects your brain*

• *Social Repair Template – reconnect without shame*

• *Burnout Barometer – catch collapse before it hits*

• *Self-Worth Log – detach your value from your productivity*

You don't need a prettier planner.

You need a system that can hold your chaos—

gently.

Chapter 8

SLEEP, SUBSTANCES & SELF-MEDICATION

WHY YOU'RE A NIGHT OWL WHO NEEDS THREE POTS OF COFFEE

BRAIN BITE: THE ADHD BRAIN AFTER DARK

Let's start with a confession:

If you've ever felt more awake at 2 a.m. than you did all day—

or chugged caffeine just to feel *barely functional*—

you're not lazy.

You're not broken.

You're just wired differently.

This isn't bad habits.

It's biology.

Specifically: a delayed circadian rhythm, a nervous system that refuses to chill,

and a brain that's always looking for something— *anything*—to regulate itself.

This chapter isn't about perfect routines you'll never stick to.

It's about what's *real*:

Sleep chaos.

Dopamine survival.

The weird tools we use just to stay standing.

If your sleep is trash and your coffee order could double as a science experiment—

you're not failing.

You're adapting.

Now let's find a way to work with it—without shame, without panic,

and without another 2 a.m. scroll titled "how to fix my brain."

PERSONAL VIGNETTE: THE NIGHTTIME BRAIN PARTY

It's late.

Nathan's asleep.

The house is quiet.

And my brain?

Wide. Freaking. Awake.

Not just awake—*thriving*.

I'm editing this book like a literary detective.

Every sentence demands attention.

Every old idea gets a shiny new upgrade.

My thoughts flicker like caffeinated fireflies:

- Plot twists

- Bonus sections

- Travel plans

- Emotional rewrites of conversations I had three years ago

Sleep stands off to the side, politely reminding me it exists.

But my ADHD brain?

It's at the party.

The prime-time brainstorm zone includes:

- Replaying awkward convos

- Planning weekend escapes

- Googling flights I won't book

By 3 a.m., I'm still going.

By 5 a.m., I crash.

And morning hits like a truck.

Because I didn't sleep.

Again.

This is the ADHD sleep paradox:

- All day = sluggish

- Nighttime = full-blown thought tornado

No amount of *"just go to bed earlier"* helps.

We don't power down on command.

We crash.

Or spiral.

Then crash harder.

DELAYED SLEEP PHASE: WHEN NIGHT FEELS LIKE HOME

Most people wind down when it gets dark.

ADHDers?

That's when the brain *turns on*.

You're not choosing to be a night owl.

Your body is just running on a different internal clock.

ADHD is strongly linked to *Delayed Sleep Phase Syndrome—*

your melatonin release comes hours late *(Coogan & McGowan, 2017).*

A randomized controlled trial found that 0.5 mg of melatonin taken early evening:

• Shifted sleep onset nearly 90 minutes earlier

• Reduced ADHD symptom severity *(van Andel et al., 2021)*

This isn't attitude.

It's clock misalignment.

If your brain finally wants to write a novel at midnight,

that's not broken.

That's biology.

Let's work with it.

• • •

WHAT SLEEP REALLY LOOKS LIKE IN ADHD

Let's go deeper than *"I'm tired."*

Sleep studies show ADHDers experience *(Sobanski et al., 2008):*

• Restless movement

• Frequent micro-awakenings

• Reduced REM

• Lower sleep efficiency

You might be *in bed* for 8 hours

and only actually *sleep* 5 or 6.

You wake up foggy.

You're already mad at yourself.

And the day hasn't started.

This isn't laziness.

It's fragmented sleep architecture.

BRIGHT LIGHT THERAPY: REWIRING YOUR CLOCK

What if you could shift your brain's clock—

not with pressure,

but with light?

A study using bright light therapy showed that consistent morning light:

• Shifted melatonin earlier by 30+ minutes

• Improved ADHD symptoms dramatically *(Fargason et al., 2017)*

Why?

Because light tells your brain:

"It's daytime now."

Your nervous system stops guessing.

And your body finally gets the message.

This isn't discipline.

It's rhythm support.

CAFFEINE, NICOTINE, SUGAR: THE LEGAL SELF-MEDS

Let's talk about survival tools.

When you're running low on dopamine, norepinephrine, and sleep?

You grab what spikes it.

• Caffeine

• Sugar

• Nicotine

• Red Bull with a side of anxiety

Why?

Because these things briefly trigger the chemicals your brain *underproduces*.

That's not weak.

That's neurochemical triage.

Research shows ADHD brains are hypersensitive to phasic dopamine—

the fast kind that comes from novelty *(Del Campo et al., 2011)*.

Caffeine works—

until it wrecks your sleep.

Sugar gives you a jolt—

until it crashes your mood.

Nicotine builds dependency—

but brings temporary calm.

These aren't vices.

They're hacks.

They're also traps.

You're not choosing bad behavior.

You're managing an unregulated system

with whatever tools you can reach.

. . .

SUBSTANCE USE: WHEN SELF-MEDICATION BECOMES A TRAP

Here's the uncomfortable truth:

ADHD significantly raises the risk of substance use disorders.

One study found that those diagnosed in childhood are far more likely to use—and misuse—substances *(Lee et al., 2011):*

• Nicotine

• Cannabis

• Cocaine

• Alcohol

• Prescription stimulants

Why?

Because substances offer:

• Stimulation

• Calm

• Focus

• Escape

This doesn't mean every ADHDer will struggle with addiction.

But without understanding or support?

The risk goes way up.

Especially when:

• You're masking all day

• Your sleep is broken

• Your nervous system is fried

THE LOOP: ADHD → SLEEP ISSUES → EXHAUSTION → SELF-MEDS → MORE ADHD

If this sounds familiar, it's because it is:

• You can't fall asleep

• You wake up tired

• You reach for caffeine

• You crash

• You grab sugar

• You mask and over-function

• You overwork at night

• You can't sleep again

Repeat.

This isn't a personal failure.

It's a survival loop.

And no one told you.

Until now.

WHAT THIS REALLY MEANS

Your late-night spirals?

Your espresso cravings?

Your endless scrolls?

They all come from one place:

A brain that's trying to regulate

itself.

Your system isn't trying to ruin your life.

It's trying to keep you stable.

Even if the methods are chaotic.

This is not sabotage.

It's survival.

You don't need more shame.

You need systems that actually support your nervous system.

You need rhythm that respects your wiring.

Recovery that doesn't feel like punishment.

And rest that doesn't feel like failure.

WHERE DO WE GO FROM HERE?

Core Insight:

Your bedtime rebellion isn't bad behavior.

It's your body trying to survive the day.

What now → Flip to Part 3, Chapter 8 for:

• *Melatonin Reset Button – shift your rhythm gently*

• *Bright Light as a Brain Anchor – use daylight, not doomscrolls*

• *20-Minute Power Reset – rest without pressure*

• *Dopamine Replacement Plan – swap chaos-coping for calm hits*

• *Sensory Wind-Down Menu – create a bedtime that loves your system*

Rest isn't weakness.

It's regulation.

Chapter 9

ADHD & COMORBIDITIES

THE B-LIST CAST OF ANXIETY, DEPRESSION & MORE

BRAIN BITE: WHEN IT'S NOT JUST ADHD—BUT IT'S ALSO STILL ADHD

So, you finally get the ADHD diagnosis.

You have a name for it.

A reason.

A flashlight in the fog.

And for a second, everything clicks.

But then... something still feels off.

Maybe the anxiety won't shut up.

Maybe your mood goes from *"I could run a company"* to *"I am the company's biggest failure"* by lunch.

Maybe your eating is all over the place.

Maybe sensory overload turns you into a ghost in your own body.

Or maybe focus was just *one slice* of the chaotic pie.

That's because ADHD rarely travels alone.

For many of us, it's the headliner in a neurodivergent ensemble cast.

Research shows that up to 50% of people with ADHD also meet criteria for at least one other psychiatric condition—and often more.

That's not because you're falling apart.

It's because the neurological systems that manage attention also touch:

• Mood

• Emotion

• Hunger

• Social processing

• Energy

• Stress response

In other words—it's not a glitch.

It's the wiring.

If your brain feels more like a group chat than a single thought stream,

you are not broken.

You are not "making excuses."

You're living in a brain that was never built for one label.

This chapter is your backstage pass—

to what else might be shaping your ADHD experience, and why knowing that changes *everything*.

PERSONAL VIGNETTE: THE STORM OF ANXIETY & THE DEPTHS OF DEPRESSION

Anxiety: The New Mom Spiral

The day I became a mom, my world split in two.

One half: awe.

A tiny human in my arms.

My heart beating outside my body.

The other half: sheer panic.

Would I lose myself in motherhood?

Would I fail?

The anxiety didn't shout. It hummed.

Low and constant—until it roared.

My ADHD brain, already a hurricane of thought, latched onto every "what if"

and spun out.

Endless spirals.

Would I ever be "me" again?

Was "me" already gone?

ADHD + anxiety = a mental ping-pong match,

bouncing between 1,000 worries.

Convinced catastrophe was always one step ahead.

Motherhood wasn't just overwhelming.

It was overstimulating.

Identity-splitting.

Emotionally endless.

And my brain had no off switch.

Depression: The Perfectionism Trap

Then came the crash.

I had been chasing a dream—outlining courses, launching ideas, writing this book.

But perfectionism crept in.

"Am I missing something?"

"What if someone else already did this better?"

"What if it's not perfect?"

Hyperfocus became obsession.

Then burnout.

I couldn't open the file.

Couldn't write.

Couldn't even *look* at what I had made.

My brain—the same one that once buzzed with vision —now whispered:

"Why bother? You're not enough."

Anxiety told me I was behind.

Perfectionism froze me.

Depression whispered: *"Why try at all?"*

Eventually, self-awareness became a rope I grabbed in the dark.

Not to escape the storm—

but to survive inside it.

TRAUMA & PTSD: THE NERVOUS SYSTEM ON ALERT

Let's start with the one we skip too often:

Trauma.

Because a lot of us with ADHD carry it—

and we're told ADHD "explains enough."

But it doesn't.

Impulsivity, emotional intensity, and poor regulation

make us more vulnerable.

More likely to be harmed.

Less likely to recover easily.

Stein et al. (2013) found that nearly 15% of PTSD cases involve dissociation—

that fuzzy, spaced-out feeling that looks like daydreaming... but isn't.

It's not distraction.

It's survival.

ADHD raises trauma risk because:

• We jump without assessing

• We feel everything louder

• We struggle to process stress

• Our bodies stay on high alert

Both ADHD and PTSD involve a sensitized HPA axis—your stress system.

When you "can't calm down" even when things are fine?

That's not drama.

That's physiology.

ANXIETY & DEPRESSION: THE OVERLOADED SYSTEM

Let's talk about the co-stars.

Studies show that 30–50% of ADHDers also struggle with anxiety or depression *(D'Agati et al., 2019)*.

Because it's exhausting—

to constantly chase focus, dodge shame, manage time, suppress emotion.

You're not just tired.

You're overstimulated and under-supported.

The science: prefrontal-limbic dysregulation.

Your rational and emotional systems are out of sync.

That's why:

• Worry loops won't stop

• Shutdowns come out of nowhere

- Guilt rides under everything

- Sadness doesn't feel clean—it feels *cluttered*

ADHD depression isn't numb.

It's messy.

Loud.

Frustrated.

Tired.

It's grief for no reason

and motivation laced with shame.

BIPOLAR DISORDER VS. ADHD: NOT THE SAME RIDE

Yes, ADHD comes with mood swings.

But bipolar?

Different arc.

Different rhythm.

Different root.

Biederman et al. (1991) explains it like this:

- ADHD: fast flips, reactive, external

- Bipolar: slow episodes, internal, patterned

In ADHD, you can flip ten moods before lunch.

In bipolar, it's days or weeks.

The confusion is understandable—

but the treatment difference is life-changing.

AUTISM SPECTRUM DISORDERS (ASD): THE OVERLAP ZONE

ADHD and autism can dance in similar spaces.

Studies estimate that 20–30% of ADHDers may meet criteria for ASD; *Craig et al. (2015)* confirms the clinical overlap and shared traits between both.

Shared traits:

• Sensory sensitivity

• Emotional intensity

• Executive dysfunction

• Rigid thinking

• Social fatigue

But:

• ADHD = craves novelty

• ASD = craves structure

You're not one or the other.

You might be both.

And that matters for how you're supported.

. . .

OCD: PERFECTIONISM ON OVERDRIVE

OCD is not "being tidy."

It's needing certainty.

When it overlaps with ADHD, it's not quirky—it's paralyzing.

You get:

• ADHD's chaos

• OCD's control

• A brain stuck in between

Brem et al. (2014) explains: both involve the prefrontal–cingulate–striatal circuit.

But they show up differently:

• ADHD = impulsive, scattered

• OCD = obsessive, stuck

Together?

• Too disorganized to start

• Too obsessive to stop

This isn't being "detail-oriented."

It's survival mode.

EATING DISORDERS: FUEL, CONTROL, EMOTION

Food isn't just fuel.

It's:

• Dopamine

• Comfort

• Rebellion

• Numbness

• Control

• A reward

• A punishment

• A break in the storm

Levin & Rawana (2016) found that ADHD—especially in women and AFAB folks—is linked to higher rates of disordered eating.

This isn't about willpower.

It's about self-regulation and emotional load.

When food becomes your nervous system's only tool—

of course it gets complicated.

You're not out of control.

You're under-supported.

.   .   .

CO-WHAT? WHY THIS ALL MATTERS

If you're reading this and thinking:

"Wait... this is all me,"

you're not broken.

You're not collecting diagnoses.

You're connecting dots.

These comorbidities don't cancel out your ADHD.

They explain it more clearly.

They shape how it shows up.

They show what you really need.

When they go unspoken,

ADHD treatment can feel like fixing a flood with a Band-Aid.

But when they're seen, named, supported?

Everything shifts.

Your brain isn't a disaster.

It's complex.

Multilingual.

Brilliant.

It just needs tools that speak all your languages.

WHERE DO WE GO FROM HERE?

Core Insight:

If the tools aren't working, it's not you—

it's the overlap.

What now → Flip to Part 3, Chapter 9 for:

• *Whole-Brain Reflection Map – name what's really happening beneath the spiral*

• *Trauma-Informed Safety Ritual – build safety into your body, not just your schedule*

• *Loop-Breaker for OCD & Perfectionism – interrupt the all-or-nothing autopilot*

• *Food Feelings Tracker – tune into your hunger, not just your habits*

• *Self-Advocacy Starter Page – ask for what you need without shrinking*

• *Neuroplasticity – rewire the story, the spiral, and the spark*

You don't need to split yourself into labels.

You just need tools that hold all your layers.

Chapter 10

ADHD IS REAL. LET'S KILL THE MYTHS

YOUR FAMILY'S FAVORITE
MISCONCEPTIONS, DEBUNKED

BRAIN BITE: LIES WE'VE BEEN TOLD—AND THE SCIENCE THAT SHUTS THEM DOWN

Let's be real:

ADHD might be one of the most misunderstood conditions in all of mental health.

Even with decades of solid neuroscience, clinical research, and lived experience from millions of people around the world,

the myths just won't die.

Why?

Because stigma has a louder voice than science.

And shame? Shame's a damn megaphone.

If you've ever been told:

- *"You just need to try harder."*

- *"You're lazy."*

- *"You're overreacting."*

- *"It's just a phase."*

- *"Everyone feels that way sometimes."*

Then yeah—

you are allowed to feel angry.

Or exhausted.

Or both.

Because no matter how hard you've tried to explain it, justify it, prove it—

someone probably made you feel like you were making excuses.

You weren't.

You were trying to describe a brain they never took the time to understand.

This chapter?

It's your scientific armor.

Your emotional validation.

Your permission slip to stop apologizing for a neurological condition you never chose.

We're not here to convince skeptics.

We're here to hand you facts—

and help you finally stop internalizing fiction.

Let's break these myths wide open.

PERSONAL VIGNETTE: THE MYTH OF ADHD — LATE DIAGNOSIS AND FINDING MY OWN PATH

I was already an adult when I finally discovered what had been powering my brain all along:

ADHD, combined type—both inattentive and hyperactive.

Suddenly, everything made sense:

- The hyperfixations

- The burnout loop

- The impulsive decisions

- The whiplash between brilliance and breakdown

But growing up?

ADHD wasn't even a blip on the radar.

In my house, you either did things well... or you didn't do them at all.

"Scattered focus" or "can't sit still" weren't conditions.

They were things you got punished for.

My parents didn't know what ADHD was.

They just saw a serial hobby-hopper.

One day I was singing and dancing.

Next, I was into swimming.

Then guitar.

Then kickboxing.

Switching sports, switching dreams—like my brain was on a never-ending dopamine scavenger hunt.

They wanted me to master one thing.

I wanted to try *everything*.

Bored and Bullied — A Classic ADHD Combo

School wasn't better.

My high school English teacher loathed my pronunciation—

but instead of helping me, she chose public humiliation.

She hated that I moved too much.

That my head drifted.

That I didn't adore her slow, posh, performative "Cambridge" accent layered on top of her Polish one.

So I made a vow:

I'd learn English *my own way*.

No textbooks.

No grammar drills.

Just real life. ADHD-style: immersive, obsessive, hyperfocused.

Fast Forward: Hyperfocus Wins Again

Years later, I moved to an English-speaking country.

No plan. No formal training.

Just me, my ADHD brain, and the need to prove something.

Eventually, I enrolled at Cambridge Regional College.

Earned my final diploma.

Became fluent.

Not with the "perfect" accent.

Just one that's *mine*.

This is what so many people miss about ADHD:

• We're not lazy—we thrive in high-interest, high-stimulation spaces.

• We're not unfocused—we're intensely focused *when it matters to us*.

• We don't "need to try harder." We need to work *with* our brains, not against them.

Growing up, I felt like I couldn't finish anything.

But I wasn't broken.

I was just following a very ADHD path to mastery:

Not linear.

Not traditional.

But absolutely powerful.

MYTH 1: ADHD IS JUST A KID THING

Spoiler: You don't grow out of ADHD.

You just get better at masking.

Turgay et al. (2012) found that about two-thirds of children with ADHD continue to experience symptoms into adulthood.

That doesn't mean they all still qualify for a full diagnosis—

it means the brain wiring doesn't magically shift.

The symptoms evolve:

• Less climbing furniture

• More missed emails

• Less blurting

• More burnout

But the executive dysfunction? Still there.

And now, it's trying to manage:

• Jobs

• Bills

• Parenting

• Everything else

Adult ADHD isn't immaturity.

It's misdiagnosed survival.

. . .

MYTH 2: YOU'RE JUST LAZY

Let's dismantle this one with science and fury.

Beaton et al. (2022) found that ADHDers are often labeled lazy—

not because they lack care,

but because they struggle with initiation, timing, and structure.

Laziness implies you *could*... and just don't.

ADHD is:

You want to. You try to. Your brain won't let you.

This isn't moral failure.

It's neurological misfiring.

You're not lazy.

You're tired of trying to prove you're not.

MYTH 3: IT'S CAUSED BY SUGAR, SCREENS, OR BAD PARENTING

No.

Still no.

Forever no.

A massive meta-analysis *(Sonuga-Barke et al., 2013)* found no solid evidence that sugar, screens, or parenting cause ADHD.

They may influence behavior—sure.

But the root?

Is genetic. Biological. Neurochemical.

This isn't a discipline issue.

It's a dopamine and regulation system issue.

MYTH 4: GIRLS DON'T GET ADHD

They do.

They just don't get *noticed*.

Girls and AFAB individuals often present with:

• Perfectionism

• Daydreaming

• People-pleasing

• Internalized shame

Quinn & Madhoo (2014) found girls are misdiagnosed or overlooked entirely.

Instead of ADHD, they're labeled:

• "Sensitive"

• "Too emotional"

• "High-functioning but scattered"

By adulthood, many are breaking down—

behind perfectly polite masks.

This isn't a symptom gap.

It's a *recognition* gap.

MYTH 5: EVERYONE'S A LITTLE ADHD

This one cuts the deepest.

It sounds like empathy.

But it minimizes disability.

According to a global meta-analysis *(Song et al., 2021)*:

• 2.58% of adults meet the full diagnostic criteria for persistent ADHD (with childhood onset)

• 6.76% experience symptomatic ADHD—they live with impairing traits, even if not fully diagnosed

That's not *"a little distracted."*

That's hundreds of millions of people struggling in silence.

Yes, everyone forgets stuff.

But not everyone:

• Misses work from task paralysis

- Ghosts loved ones out of shame

- Feels time like soup instead of structure

- Melts down over one last thing

- Lives in a spiral of over-commit, under-deliver, crash, restart

That's not quirky.

That's ADHD.

And it's real.

ADHD IS NOT AN EXCUSE—IT'S AN EXPLANATION

Saying *"I have ADHD"* isn't a cop-out.

It's a map.

A way to understand the terrain of your brain

so you can stop fighting it

and start building systems that work *with it*.

This isn't about lowering standards.

It's about ditching shame.

You don't need to convince anyone anymore.

But when the gaslighting gets loud—inside or out—

this chapter is your shield.

You're not dramatic.

You're not lazy.

You're telling the truth.

And now?

You've got the science to back it up.

WHERE DO WE GO FROM HERE?

Core Insight:

You don't have to prove ADHD is real anymore.

You get to protect your truth.

What now → Flip to Part 3, Chapter 10 for:

• *Myth-Buster Scripts – science-backed responses for every myth*

• *Internalized Shame Decoder – rewrite the lies stuck in your head*

• *Emotional Self-Advocacy Scripts – speak your truth with zero apology*

• *Energy-Protection Boundary Plan – say less, protect more*

• *Community Building Starter Pack – find your people or create your circle*

You don't need to argue anymore.

You just need to root in what's real.

Chapter 11

ADHD IS ALSO A SUPERPOWER

YES, REALLY

BRAIN BITE: THE BRILLIANCE BENEATH THE BUZZ

By now, you've made it through the thick of it:

- The executive dysfunction

- The rejection spirals

- The late-night chaos

- The dopamine droughts

- The shame

- The shutdowns

- The missed calls

- The internal voice that never lets up

But that's not the whole story.

This chapter is about the other side.

The side of ADHD that doesn't get talked about in therapy offices, report cards, or performance reviews.

The side where the same wiring that makes life hard in one context

makes you *magnetic* in another.

This isn't "everyone's special" fluff.

This is real, research-backed brilliance that shows up again and again in ADHD brains.

Because for every challenge, there's also a pattern of power

that deserves to be named—

and claimed.

So if you've ever felt like a:

• Misfit genius

• Chaos-loving visionary

• Deep feeler with fast-twitch intuition

• Last-minute miracle worker

• Idea machine

• Comeback kid

• Problem-solver in panic mode

• Late bloomer with Big Energy™

You're not making it up.

You're not "just compensating."

You're not being dramatic.

You are wired for intensity.

And when that intensity is understood and supported?

It becomes:

- Creativity

- Empathy

- Humor

- Resilience

- Insight

This chapter is here to name it all.

Not to erase the hard stuff—

but to *complete the picture.*

You're not just struggling.

You're also *exceptional.*

Let's talk about what Brain 2.0 is *actually* built to do well—

not in theory, but in real life.

PERSONAL VIGNETTE: THE SPARK THAT UNLEASHED MY SUPERPOWER

I'll never forget the day I took my first ADHD med.

Not to "fix" myself—

but because I was stuck in the loop.

Endless inspiration.

Zero activation.

My brain held ideas like constellations,

but everything I dreamed kept slamming into a wall.

Then one quiet afternoon—

Nathan building a Lego Technic Lambo at my feet,

sunlight dancing across the floor—

I took that first dose.

And something shifted.

The fog lifted.

The gate opened.

Tasks I'd abandoned at Step One began unfolding.

One by one.

Writing.

Editing.

Crafting nuanced chapters.

They all became my hyperfocus playground.

That moment wasn't about being fixed.

It was about being *free*.

I channeled that energy into this book.

Wove childhood memories, my son's mirrored struggles, and the science we both needed

into something that could *actually* help people.

Chapter after chapter flowed—

not perfectly,

but powerfully.

Fueled by the joy of finally building something for

every ADHD soul who's ever been told they were "too much" or "not enough."

That moment?

That was my superpower awakening.

ADHD isn't a hurdle.

It's a launchpad.

My hyperfocus became my engine.

My resilience, my compass.

And my creativity?

My gift to the world.

This book isn't just healing for me.

It's a love letter to you—

proof that once you understand your wiring,

your so-called *quirks* become your greatest strength.

CREATIVITY & DIVERGENT THINKING: YOUR UNINHIBITED IMAGINATION

That thing where your brain:

• Interrupts itself

• Jumps topics

• Pivots mid-sentence

• Connects five ideas before speaking one

Yeah. That's the magic.

White & Shah (2006) found that ADHDers outperform neurotypicals on divergent thinking tasks—

especially the "Unusual Uses Task."

We crushed it.

Why?

Because we have:

• Lower inhibition (we don't block the "weird" ideas)

• More active default mode networks (wandering = imagination)

• Faster associative thinking (we connect dots others can't see)

You're not random.

You're original.

• • •

HYPERFOCUS: YOUR ZONE OF POWER

People say ADHD means you can't focus.

But when the conditions are right?

We don't just focus.

We *disappear* into the work.

Hupfeld et al. (2019) validated this: ADHDers experience more frequent, productive hyperfocus episodes

than the average brain.

This is your tunnel state.

Your creative trance.

Not everyone has access to this kind of flow.

You do.

It's not a deficit.

It's *regulation*.

And when it aligns?

You're unstoppable.

RESILIENCE: THE BOUNCE-FORWARD BRAIN

ADHD makes life harder.

That's a fact.

But it also forges us in fire.

Regalla et al. (2019) found that ADHDers may score lower on resilience early on—

but when supported,

we bounce back *hard*.

Why?

Because we've already:

• Rebuilt after misunderstanding

• Pivoted inside broken systems

• Survived 1,000 "too much"s

• Failed, adapted, and tried again

Our resilience isn't loud.

It's earned.

It's creative.

It's gritty.

We don't just bounce back.

We bounce *forward*.

EMPATHY & EMOTIONAL DEPTH

People say ADHD means "you don't pay attention."

But we *feel* everything.

Shaw et al. (2014) showed that ADHD brains are hyper-attuned to emotional signals—

even when we struggle to regulate them.

That's why we:

• Pick up on moods before words are spoken

• Cry easily and deeply

• Feel the energy shift in a room before anyone else notices

This isn't fragility.

It's *emotional fluency.*

It's why we lead with heart.

Why we show up for people.

Why our presence is *felt.*

And when we protect that depth?

It becomes a force.

HUMOR, ENERGY & MOMENTUM

Need someone to flip the mood?

Say the line that makes everyone exhale?

That's us.

Beaton et al. (2022) found that adults with ADHD often use humor, wit, and quick emotional reading as social tools—to cope with criticism, soften connection, and protect their sense of self.

We notice the energy shift.

We read the room before the words arrive.

We use humor to bond, to buffer, to say what no one else can quite name.

We are wired for:

• The absurd link

• The sharp punchline

• The laugh that heals something quiet inside

We joke to survive.

To connect.

To reclaim our worth in spaces that don't always see us clearly.

Our humor isn't random.

It's emotional insight in motion.

ENTREPRENEURIAL & LEADERSHIP POTENTIAL

You know the person who:

• Can't sit still

• Starts five things at once

• Breaks rules and reinvents the wheel?

That's not dysfunction.

That's vision.

Verheul et al. (2016) found that hyperactive ADHDers are more likely to become self-employed.

Because we:

- Hate red tape

- Crave autonomy

- Create under pressure

- Don't wait to be invited—we build the room

We don't always *fit* the system.

But we often *improve* it.

THE SUPERPOWER IS REAL—WHEN UNDERSTOOD

Let's get real:

This isn't "ADHD is a gift."

It's:

ADHD is powerful *when seen, supported, and unshamed.*

When ignored?

It wrecks you.

When shamed?

It burns you out.

When masked?

It steals your spark.

But when understood?

It becomes:

• Innovation

• Comedy

• Art

• Empathy

• Leadership

• Healing

• Movement

• Change

Your brain isn't broken.

It's different.

You're not here to blend in.

You're here to *shift* the shape of the world.

WHERE DO WE GO FROM HERE?

Core Insight:

Your fire isn't the problem.

It's the *plan*.

What now → Flip to Part 3, Chapter 11 for:

• *Hyperfocus Goal Sprint Map – use your fire without burnout*

• *Flow State Setup & Disruption Shield – protect your zone*

• *Resilience + Joy Journal – log the bounce forward*

• *Strengths → Career Bridge – align your work to your wiring*

• *Creative Confidence Reframe Deck – your weird is your superpower*

You don't need to become someone else to thrive.

You just need to unleash what was always there.

And if you're still wondering what that kind of brain can really do?

Let's meet 15 of the most brilliant, bold, and beautifully neurodivergent minds

who didn't just survive the storm—

they changed the world with it.

BONUS CHAPTER: NEURODIVERGENT MINDS WHO CHANGED THE WORLD

THE POWER OF THINKING DIFFERENTLY

This chapter is a celebration of real minds that reshaped the world.

Some were confirmed neurodivergent.

Some are widely considered to have been.

All of them made their mark not in spite of how they think—

but because of it.

We begin with historical icons.

They were never formally diagnosed,

but are often referenced in neurodivergent circles for their brilliance, eccentricity, and nonlinear genius.

Then we meet modern changemakers—

people who have confirmed their diagnosis and redefined what it means to succeed on your own terms.

This chapter isn't about labels.

It's about possibility.

HISTORICALLY CONSIDERED NEURODIVERGENT

While these individuals were never formally diagnosed, many scholars and biographers have retrospectively identified traits consistent with ADHD or related neurodivergent profiles.

Albert Einstein – Theoretical Physicist

Revolutionized physics with his theory of relativity.

Einstein famously struggled in traditional schooling, was often described as disorganized and distractible, and preferred independent thinking over structured systems.

Many modern articles and ADHD advocates point to his pattern of hyperfocus, impulsivity, and sensory-seeking behaviors—like intense solitude and complex thought experiments—as resonant with ADHD traits.

While there is no formal diagnosis, and all interpretations are retrospective, his story remains one of the most commonly cited in conversations about neurodivergent brilliance.

(*SciJournal.org – "Famous Scientists with ADHD"*)

Benjamin Franklin – Founding Father and Inventor

Invented the lightning rod. Helped frame the U.S. Constitution. Founded a library, a university, and a fire department.

Franklin was known for his insatiable curiosity, constant reinvention, and difficulty following routines —even ones he set for himself.

In his own writing, he described the struggle to stick to schedules and complete habits, despite immense drive and output.

Mental health experts, including clinicians at Mayo Clinic, have cited Franklin as one of several brilliant historical figures believed to have exhibited traits consistent with ADHD.

While there is no formal diagnosis, his legacy is often discussed in neurodivergent circles as a symbol of nonlinear genius and creative momentum.

(*Mayo Clinic Health System – "What is ADHD?"*)

Leonardo da Vinci – Polymath

Inventor. Artist. Anatomist. Visionary.

Leonardo left behind a trail of unfinished projects— yet still produced some of the most revolutionary art and design in history.

A 2019 peer-reviewed article in *Brain* suggests Leonardo's struggles with task completion, time management, and chronic procrastination reflect what we now understand as core ADHD traits.

He was known for his relentless curiosity, nonlinear work style, and bursts of intense creative focus followed by long gaps and sudden pivots.

His own notebooks hint at frustration. He juggled dozens of ideas at once, rarely satisfied, always chasing the next vision.

While there is no formal diagnosis, the article concludes that ADHD offers the most scientifically grounded explanation for Leonardo's extraordinary brilliance and scattered execution.

(*Brain Journal – "Leonardo da Vinci: A Genius Driven by Distraction"*)

CONFIRMED NEURODIVERGENT MINDS

These individuals have publicly confirmed an ADHD or autism diagnosis and changed the world by being fully themselves.

Elon Musk – Entrepreneur

Disrupted the automotive, space, and tech industries.

From Tesla to SpaceX to Neuralink, Musk has pushed humanity forward.

He confirmed his autism diagnosis (formerly Asperger's) on *Saturday Night Live* in 2021.

(*BBC News – "Elon Musk reveals he has Asperger's on Saturday Night Live"*)

Richard Branson – Entrepreneur

Founder of the Virgin Group and pioneer in aviation, music, and space tourism.

Branson has openly discussed living with ADHD and dyslexia.

He attributes his creative problem-solving and risk-taking to his neurodivergent brain.

(*Edge Foundation – "Sir Richard Branson – ADHD Entrepreneur Extraordinaire"*)

Michael Phelps – Olympic Swimmer

The most decorated Olympian in history, with 28 medals.

Diagnosed with ADHD at age 9, Phelps credits swimming with helping him manage focus and energy.

His story redefined ADHD in the public eye.

(*ADDitude Magazine – "How Swimming Saved Michael Phelps: An ADHD Story"*)

Simone Biles – Gymnast

A record-breaking force in gymnastics and beyond.

Biles confirmed her ADHD diagnosis after medical records were leaked in 2016, and she responded publicly with strength and advocacy.

(*ESPN – "Bravo, Simone Biles, for taking a stand against ADHD stigma"*)

Jim Carrey – Actor and Comedian

Known for explosive energy, physical humor, and emotional depth.

Carrey has spoken publicly about living with ADHD and depression, and how creativity became his outlet and regulation strategy.

(*Edge Foundation – "Jim Carrey: A Life of Color"*)

Howie Mandel – Comedian and TV Host

From *Deal or No Deal* to *America's Got Talent*, Mandel has used humor to open conversations about mental health.

He has publicly discussed both his ADHD and OCD diagnoses, helping normalize neurodivergence on mainstream platforms.

(*LDRFA – "Howie Mandel Gets Real About His ADHD and OCD"*)

THE TAKEAWAY

This list isn't just a roll call of brilliance. It's a reminder:

That neurodivergence isn't a flaw.

It's a form of intelligence.

A pattern of depth.

A fuel for impact.

You don't need to become someone else to thrive.

You just need to work with the brain you already have.

Because history doesn't get changed by the ones who blend in.

It gets changed by the ones who think differently.

WRAPPING UP PART TWO: THE TRUTH UNDERNEATH IT ALL

YOU'RE NOT BROKEN—YOU'RE BUILT DIFFERENT

TAKE A BREATH

You just walked through the heart of it—

the inner architecture of the ADHD brain.

The science.

The shame.

The sensory floods.

The spirals.

The shutdowns.

The secret superpowers.

Not just under a microscope—

but in the mirror.

This wasn't about data.

It was about truth.

The kind you feel in your chest

before your brain catches up.

WHAT YOU JUST DID

You didn't just learn about ADHD.

You reclaimed it.

Chapter by chapter, you untangled yourself from other people's stories:

- The "lazy"

- The "inconsistent"

- The "too much"

- The "not enough"

You walked straight into the hard stuff:

Executive dysfunction.

Emotional dysregulation.

Sleep spirals.

Substance loops.

Trauma overlaps.

And the myths that made you doubt yourself.

You faced it all.

And you stayed.

That's not just education.

That's integration.

WHAT THIS PART REALLY MEANT

This wasn't just a science section.

It was a translation.

It was the moment you realized:

You're not a mess.

You're a system.

You're not failing.

You're firing—

just on a frequency no one ever taught you how to tune into.

This was the map.

The wiring.

The rhythms.

The emotional weather.

The real reasons.

No shame.

No gimmicks.

Just your operating system—

finally, in your language.

THE INTELLIGENCE YOU BUILT

You built a kind of intelligence here

that doesn't show up on tests or resumes.

It's the wisdom of:

"This isn't sabotage. It's survival."

It's the power of recognizing a freeze loop

before it swallows your day.

It's self-trust.

ADHD isn't just about focus.

It's about regulation:

• Of attention

• Of emotion

• Of energy

• Of expectation

And now?

You're the one designing the system.

WHERE YOU'RE HEADING NEXT

If Part Two gave you the map,

Part Three helps you build the road.

This is where science becomes system.

Where story becomes strategy.

Where every pattern you named finally gets a tool that fits.

You've seen the storms.

Now let's ride the current.

You're not here to fix your brain.

You're here to work with it.

Part 3

BUILDING YOUR ADHD TOOLKIT — STRATEGIES THAT ACTUALLY WORK

PERSONALIZED SYSTEMS, RITUALS, AND HACKS TO HELP YOUR BRAIN THRIVE. REAL TOOLS FOR REAL ADHD LIVES.

BEFORE READING PART THREE: HOW TO USE WHAT COMES NEXT

HOW TO USE THIS TOOLKIT
(WITHOUT OVERWHELM

THIS ISN'T A CHECKLIST

It's not homework.

It's definitely not another planner you'll abandon in three days.

Part Three is a toolbox.

You don't have to use every tool.

You don't even have to read it in order.

HERE'S HOW TO APPROACH IT—ADHD STYLE

• **Start where it hurts—or where it helps**

Each chapter connects to one from Part Two.

Struggling with emotion? Go there.

Stuck at the start line? Head to executive function.

Foggy? Fiery? Frozen? Pick your flavor.

- **Take what works. Leave the rest**

These aren't rules. They're invitations.

Try a tool. Adapt it. Toss it. Return to it sideways in six months.

That's not failure.

That's ADHD-friendly progress.

- **Build your own system**

Your brain isn't broken—it's just built differently.

This part helps you build with it, not against it.

Inside, you'll find tools for:

○ Routines based on rhythm, not rigidity

○ Dopamine-fueled strategies for starting and sustaining

○ Emotional regulation, time awareness, sleep scaffolding, self-worth

○ Hacks that hold your chaos with care, not control

- **Come back when you need to**

You don't have to finish this.

You just have to find what moves you.

Bookmark the ones that land.

Highlight the ones that heal.

Skip the ones that don't—maybe they will later.

THE TURNING POINT

If you need one line to carry with you, let it be this:

You're not broken. You're built different.

And different?

Isn't something to hide.

It's something to honor.

To build with.

To lead with.

To live with.

You've named the noise.

Tracked the storms.

Learned the signals.

Now comes the shift:

From survival to strategy.

From confusion to clarity.

From coping... to creating.

Let's get into it—

gently, joyfully,

and fully on your terms.

Chapter 1

STRENGTHS & STRUGGLES MAPPING

BUILDING YOUR ADHD
OPERATING SYSTEM

OPENING GROUNDING MOMENT

Let's be honest.

You've probably downloaded 15 productivity apps, bought the planner, color-coded the tabs, and still somehow forgot the dentist appointment and the laundry in the machine. Again.

Welcome.

This chapter isn't about becoming someone else's idea of "organized."

This is the part where we stop glitching through life on someone else's Wi-Fi.

We're switching over to your home network now.

WHAT THIS CHAPTER HELPS YOU DO

This chapter helps you build a map—not a plan.

A map of how you actually work.

What lights you up. What burns you out.

And how to build a rhythm that respects your brilliance instead of betraying it.

This isn't about leveling up.

This is about syncing with your cycles, not fighting them every damn day.

You are the operating system.

Let's make it run on your settings.

TOOL 1: THE STRENGTHS & STRUGGLES MAP

How it was born (a.k.a. my napkin moment)

It was 11:00 p.m. on a Tuesday.

Nathan had just passed out mid-sentence on the couch, and my brain was spinning.

Like, brain-stuck-in-a-tornado spinning.

Why can I write 40 pages in one day but can't email the school nurse back?

Why does a color-coded planner feel like a crime scene?

I looked around: sticky notes. Cold coffee. A half-eaten Raffaello.

And then I grabbed a napkin.

I drew two columns. Not fancy. Just real.

Left column: Things that light me up

Right column: Things that flatten me

Hyperfocus surges. Creative sprints. Emotional weather.

Time blocks when I come alive (spoiler: it's not 9 a.m.).

That napkin? It was my operating system.

Not a productivity hack. Not a shame spiral. Just a mirror.

Now it's your turn.

What to do

• Grab anything: paper, notes app, your kid's old worksheet, a literal napkin

• Draw two columns:

• Strength Zones

• Drain Zones

• What to list:

• Times when you felt unstoppable (hyperfocus, flow, joy)

• Times when you couldn't move (freeze, shutdown, fog)

• Emotional patterns (shutdowns? meltdowns? burnout cycles?)

• Time-of-day rhythms

• Sensory or environmental triggers

This is not a to-do list.

It's a compassion map.

You're not inconsistent.

You're cyclical.

Let your map show you your fire—and your fog.

. . .

How it worked for me

When I first mapped out my strengths and struggles, I realized something:

I wasn't "bad" at organizing.

I was just trying to force myself into someone else's rhythm.

For example, I'm not a morning person—and no, a cute Pinterest morning routine isn't going to change that.

But once I recognized my brain's natural rhythm, I saw that my creative bursts typically happened after lunch.

So I started scheduling creative work during my high-energy windows.

Boom. The system started working for me.

"I wasn't failing. I was forcing" (Hallowell & Ratey, 2021).

TOOL 2: YOUR OS, NOT THEIR PLANNER

How it was born

I tried the Instagram routines.

You know the ones: wake at 5 a.m., gratitude journal, green juice, 17-step skincare routine, collapse by 8.

By day three, I was sobbing on the bathroom floor with a matcha latte and a crisis of identity.

Then I stopped copying—and started designing.

What to do

• Ask yourself:

• When does your brain come online?

• What time of day are you at your worst?

• Do you need sound or silence to focus?

• What spaces make you buzz? Which ones make you breathe?

Start building from that.

Not from shame.

From data. From truth. From you.

Stop asking, "How do I become consistent?"

Start asking, "What supports the rhythm I already have?"

. . .

How it worked for me

I spent years trying to wake up "like a responsible adult."

It never worked.

Then I accepted that my brain really kicks in around 11 a.m.

I'm sharpest after lunch.

So I gave my mornings low-pressure tasks—checking emails, reading, just existing.

And I saved my creative firepower for when it actually showed up.

This tool built on my map.

I stopped mapping my rhythm—and started building from it *(Barkley, 1997)*.

TOOL 3: THE DOPAMINE COMPASS

How it was born

ADHD isn't an attention deficit.

It's an attention hunger *(Volkow et al., 2009)*.

Dopamine is the thing we chase—the thing that lights us up.

How I learned this: I once forgot to pee for four hours while writing this book.

I also took 17 days and two meltdowns to call the dentist.

Now I track:

• What makes me lose time in the best way?

• What shuts me down instantly?

• What feels good in the moment but ends in shame or regret?

No charts. Just awareness.

Once you know what feeds your fire,

you can stop trying to make yourself function in a system that starves it.

How it worked for me

The biggest breakthrough?

I stopped blaming myself for procrastination.

Instead, I started tracking my dopamine spikes.

Writing this chapter? I forgot to eat. I wasn't managing time badly.

I was lit up.

Now I work in sprints—followed by movement, food, or softness.

Fuel, not force.

TOOL 4: THE "NOT BROKEN, JUST DIFFERENT" SCRIPT SET

How it was born

Sometimes the meanest voice in the room is my own.

So I started translating it.

"I'm all over the place" → "I move fast and connect dots others miss."

"I never finish anything" → "My brain works in sprints, not slogs."

These aren't affirmations.

They're truths in your language.

Say them out loud.

Whisper them in traffic.

Write them on your fridge.

Let your brain hear the version of you that knows you're not a failure.

How it worked for me

I used to shame myself for not finishing things.

Projects half-done. Ideas dropped mid-burst.

Then I reframed it:

My brain is built for sprints, not marathons *(Sarkis, 2015).*

That sentence alone softened a lifetime of self-blame.

TOOL 5: THE ADHD OS VISUALIZER

How it was born

My brain isn't broken.

It just runs a weird and wonderful operating system.

Some days I forget that.

So I draw it:

- Executive function = squirrel with a clipboard

- Emotional regulation = volcano in a tutu

- Attention = golden retriever chasing butterflies

Absurd? Yes.

But these sketches bring me home.

When I see my brain clearly,

I stop blaming it blindly.

How it worked for me

I used to feel shame when my attention wandered.

During meetings. Phone calls. Even at home.

Then I started saying:

"Oh, that's just my brain being a puppy."

And it worked.

Instead of spiraling, I redirected.

With compassion. With humor.

Visual language helped me see my brain as different, not defective *(Mahone & Denckla, 2017)*.

TRY THIS IF...

• You've tried following other people's productivity systems and they don't stick

• You keep thinking you're inconsistent—but it's really just rhythm

• You feel overwhelmed by your environment but don't know why

• You're ready to stop blaming yourself for your ADHD brain

GENTLE PRACTICE PROMPT

Tonight, write down one thing you've always been told makes you "too much."

Then ask yourself:

What if this is actually the part of me I came here to protect?

Sleep on it.

Let your truth rise.

WHAT'S NEXT

Now that you've mapped your rhythm, we move to your flavor.

Because ADHD isn't one-size-fits-anything.

And the tools shouldn't be either.

Let's go meet your flavor—foggy, fiery, fierce.

See you in **Chapter 2**.

Chapter 2

FLAVOR-SPECIFIC
STRATEGIES

FINDING YOUR RHYTHM, NOT
SOMEONE ELSE'S ROUTINE

OPENING GROUNDING MOMENT

Some days you wake up feeling like a fog bank.

Other days, like a firecracker on espresso.

And sometimes, both in the same hour.

Welcome to ADHD, aka the ultimate surprise playlist.

This chapter isn't about picking one flavor and sticking to it.

It's about realizing your brain shapeshifts—and learning to shift with it.

We're not labeling.

We're listening.

Because your ADHD isn't a diagnosis on paper.

It's a living rhythm.

And it deserves tools that move with it, not against it.

WHAT THIS CHAPTER HELPS YOU DO

This chapter helps you name the version of your brain that's showing up—today, not five years ago.

You'll learn how to tune in to your energy and adjust your rituals accordingly, without shame or self-blame.

This is about building rhythm, not routines.

It's your permission to be dynamic.

You're not inconsistent.

You're responsive.

And now your toolkit gets to be, too.

TOOL 1: FLAVOR-CHECK DIARIES

How it was born

Some days you're foggy. Others, frantic.

This isn't inconsistency—it's intelligence adapting to context *(Fassbender et al., 2015)*.

But most ADHDers never stop to name what version of themselves just walked into the room.

So I started doing it.

One tiny diary entry—one sentence each morning:

Today I feel...

• Foggy and floaty (SCT) *(Fassbender et al., 2015)*

• Like a spark plug on espresso (HI) *(Willcutt, 2012)*

• Like both at once (Combined)

• Like I'm performing calm but screaming inside (Masked AF) *(Biederman et al., 2010)*

That one sentence gave me clarity.

Not a diagnosis. A starting point.

It told me whether I needed movement or stillness. Structure or softness. Fuel or recovery.

How it worked for me

For years, I felt like my brain was either in overdrive or shut down.

Some days I was a superhero. Other days, I was frozen.

The turning point was when I stopped pushing through and started checking in.

On foggy mornings, I stopped trying to "snap out of it."

I stretched. I moved—just a little.

Enough to meet myself where I was.

On hyperactive days, I didn't try to slow down.

I gave that energy somewhere to go—creative sprints, physical movement, loud music.

The check-in didn't fix everything.

But it told me where to start.

TOOL 2: TEMPO-MATCHING STRATEGY

How it was born

Once I stopped demanding I operate like a calendar app, and started listening to my tempo, everything changed.

People with ADHD often struggle to sync with external rhythms—we can't always find our internal beat *(Puyjarinet et al., 2017).*

So I started using rhythm tools to help me find it from the outside in.

• If I was SCT-slow, I used rhythm—music, sound loops, fidget toys

• If I was hyper-buzzy, I channeled it into creative sprints—with alarms to stop

• If I was both, I let myself toggle. Pause. Pivot. Flow.

This wasn't about symptom management.

This was about nervous system design.

How it worked for me

When Nathan and I started building rhythm together, I noticed how his energy moved differently than mine —and how quickly it could change.

We created a shared system, flexible enough for both of us:

• 40-minute work bursts

• Movement breaks in between

• Tempo-matching: if he was buzzing, we'd go outside and move; if I needed quiet, I'd retreat to a nook

It wasn't rigid structure.

It was permission to move with our actual bodies.

Not against them.

Tool 1 helped me name my internal flavor.

This tool helped me respond to it in real time.

TOOL 3: MASKING AWARENESS LOG

How it was born

Most women with ADHD are never told they're masking. I wasn't.

I just thought I was "too sensitive." Or "exhausted from socializing."

Girls with ADHD are often missed entirely—not because the symptoms aren't there, but because they don't always look like what people expect *(Slobodin & Davidovitch, 2019).*

They're quieter. They're overwhelmed. And they're really, really good at pretending they're fine.

Turns out, masking drains energy faster than anything else.

So I started tracking:

• Where did I perform today?

• Where did I suppress my needs or stims?

• Where did I feel safe enough to be real?

Over time, this log became a liberation map.

A slow return to myself.

How it worked for me

I didn't realize how much I was hiding—especially as a mom trying to "hold it all together."

I smiled when I was collapsing.

I stayed silent when I needed help.

Nathan's ADHD diagnosis cracked something open.

I saw myself in his struggle. I saw my own masking.

So I began unmasking—gently.

I tracked when I was pretending.

And I gave myself permission to say, *"I'm not okay right now."*

That honesty didn't make me weaker.

It made me real.

TOOL 4: SENSORY ENVIRONMENT TUNER

How it was born

My flavor changes.

And so do my sensory thresholds.

Some days I crave stimulation.

Other days, even a whisper makes me flinch.

Sensory over-responsivity is increasingly recognized as part of ADHD—not just a side effect, but a real dimension of how we process the world *(Lane & Reynolds, 2019)*.

So I built a toolkit with options—not obligations:

- Noise-canceling headphones

- Sunglasses

- Weighted blanket

- Spotify loops

- Barefoot grounding in the garden

- Light filters

- Smells that soothe

How it worked for me

Some days I couldn't focus because of everything.

Lights too bright. Fabric too itchy. Sounds too much.

So I stopped enduring and started designing.

I made my environment a partner, not a punishment.

I added softness, dimmed lights, layered nature sounds in the background.

Nathan, a sensory seeker, needed the opposite.

So we created zones—quiet corners for me, energetic corners for him.

Now our house works with our nervous systems.

Not against them.

TOOL 5: FLAVOR-SPECIFIC MINI-PLANS

How it was born

I didn't need one master plan.

I needed five mini-plans—for five flavors of me.

ADHD doesn't just show up differently from person to person—it shapeshifts inside each of us.

That's why customizing strategies to your flavor matters *(Blanchfield, 2023)*.

So I wrote a one-pager for each:

• INATTENTIVE = chunked tasks, verbal processing, soft accountability

• HYPERACTIVE = urgency, movement, permission to sprint then rest

• COMBINED = stimulation, freedom, pivot-friendly choices

• SCT = slow starts, visual cues, gentle pacing

• MASKED = honesty, recovery, post-performance rest

These weren't rules.

They were reminders.

When I forget who I am, I reread them like love letters to my brain.

How it worked for me

I stopped asking, *"Why can't I follow through?"*

I started asking, *"Who just showed up?"*

When Nathan was hyperactive, I gave him jump zones and trampoline time.

When I was masked, I gave myself space to feel.

And when I needed to just start one load of laundry? That was enough.

My flavor wasn't a problem.

It was the context.

TRY THIS IF...

• You keep changing tools and blaming yourself instead of the mismatch

• You feel foggy when others say you're "too much"

• Your energy crashes after you've "done it all right"

• You're always the calm one in public and the exhausted one in private

• You've never fit the textbook—and that's made you feel fake

GENTLE PRACTICE PROMPT

Tonight, write:

"My ADHD doesn't have to be loud to be real.

It doesn't have to match anyone else's version to matter."

Then write how your brain showed up today.

That's enough.

WHAT'S NEXT

Now that you've mapped your flavor and stopped fighting your tempo, it's time to drop deeper—into the biology beneath the behavior.

Chapter 3 is where we open the hood.

Neurochemistry. Gut health. Cortisol storms.

This is the pulse beneath the patterns.

Let's meet your dopamine.

Chapter 3
FUEL, FLOW & FOCUS
INSIDE THE ADHD BRAIN

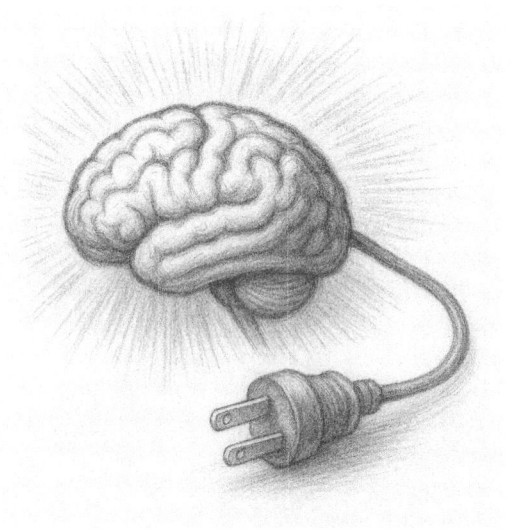

OPENING GROUNDING MOMENT

Okay, let's say it: motivation is not your moral compass.

It's brain chemistry.

If you've ever felt like a lifeless pancake one moment and a genius raccoon the next, it's not a personal failing—

It's your internal fuel system being its beautifully unpredictable self.

This chapter isn't about fixing your focus with discipline and shame.

It's about feeding your fire.

Literally. Biologically. Joyfully.

Because when you understand what your brain needs to flow,

you stop pushing, and you start surfing.

WHAT THIS CHAPTER HELPS YOU DO

This chapter helps you decode your energy cycles,

stop blaming yourself for every crash,

and learn how to feed your dopamine

without living in a caffeine loop or sugar spiral.

It gives you simple rituals—

not just hacks—

to regulate your rhythm,

reset your spark,

and move through your day

with less burnout and more brilliance.

You don't need more pressure.

You need better fuel.

Let's light it up.

TOOL 1: THE DOPAMINE-FIRST MORNING FLOW

How it was born

For years, I had no clue my mental engine was basically stuck on "low battery."

Then I learned about dopamine—and everything changed.

I rebuilt my mornings from scratch.

Here's what I used to do:

Open phone. Chug coffee. Scroll social media.

Wonder why I was spiraling by 10 a.m.

Here's what I do now:

• Cold splash or shower

• Light—natural if possible

• Gentle or hardcore movement (depends on my flavor of the day)

• Then coffee

• Late-morning, protein-rich breakfast—around 11 a.m.

It sounds small. It is small.

But it rewires everything.

This tool isn't about what you eat or do—it's about when you do it.

It's the order of ignition.

I stopped forcing motivation. I started building it
(Fargason et al., 2017).

Try this tomorrow morning:

- Drink something cold

- Touch sunlight for 3 minutes

- Move your body for 30 seconds

- Then decide what matters today

How it worked for me

My mornings used to be chaos:

Scrolling in bed. Skipping meals. Coffee on an empty
stomach.

Then I'd crash by noon, confused and shaky.

Now I treat mornings like ignition:

- Cold water to wake up my nervous system

- Ten minutes of sunlight

- Movement—any kind

I call it Morning Melt when it's gentle yoga or stretch
+ sun.

Espresso Legs if I blast music and dance like
nobody's watching.

ADHD Power Walk when I pace in circles and imagine my next chapter.

Sometimes it's jumping jacks in my pajamas.

Sometimes it's air squats while brushing my teeth.

No rules. Just rhythm.

Because movement doesn't just help me feel good—

It helps me be me.

Exercise releases dopamine, norepinephrine, and serotonin—

the very neurotransmitters ADHD brains struggle to regulate *(Ratey, 2024)*.

After movement comes coffee—my second ignition key.

Then a real breakfast—protein-rich and brain-ready.

When I actually give my brain what it needs to wake up,

I don't have to battle it for hours.

TOOL 2: FOOD AS A DOPAMINE PHARMACY

How it was born

If Tool 1 is about *when* and *how* to start the day,

this one is about what you put in the tank.

Once upon a time, I ate like a distracted toddler.

Now, food is my prescription.

Dopamine needs tyrosine.

Tyrosine comes from protein.

Protein starts with breakfast (*Morgan, 2024*).

ADHD isn't cured by a smoothie—

But it can absolutely be stabilized by real nourishment.

My go-tos:

• Boiled eggs + avocado + sauerkraut

• Greek yogurt + berries + almonds

• Pumpkin seeds + dark chocolate

• Salmon + sweet potato lunch with Nathan (his favorite) at 2 p.m.—his post-med "real meal"

This isn't a diet.

It's support.

It's scaffolding.

It's regulation through nourishment.

How it worked for me

I used to think my brain was just "wired differently,"

and that I was stuck with chaotic eating patterns that made things harder.

But once I got intentional with my food, it was like I had flipped a switch.

I stopped skipping meals.

I started eating protein-rich foods with every meal.

I took time to eat slowly—something I had never done before.

When I ate well, I felt more regulated, more present,

and far less like my brain was trapped on a caffeine-fueled roller coaster.

TOOL 3: THE GUT-BRAIN DOPAMINE TRACKER

How it was born

If Tool 2 is about fueling the engine,

this one is about listening to the engine light.

I used to think my anxiety was emotional.

Sometimes it is.

But sometimes... it's inflammation.

Gut health and dopamine are besties.

Most of your serotonin and a ton of dopamine precursors are made in your gut *(Levy Schwartz et al., 2024).*

I started noticing:

• When I ate too much sugar, I crashed

• When I ate fermented foods, I focused

• When I skipped fiber, I spiraled

So I made a simple tracker:

What I ate → How I felt → What I noticed

Yogurt helps.

Probiotics help.

Water helps.

Sauerkraut (weirdly) helps.

Your gut isn't just digestion.

It's your co-pilot.

And ADHD? It listens.

How it worked for me

I used to be completely unaware of the connection between my gut and my brain.

But once I began tracking what I ate and how I felt, the patterns were undeniable.

Processed food or sugar? Foggy, agitated, drained.

Fermented foods or probiotics? Focused, connected, calmer.

My body was talking.

All I had to do was listen—

and feed it well.

TOOL 4: CORTISOL RESET LOOPS

How it was born

Here's what happens:

A vague email hits your inbox.

Your chest tightens. You freeze.

Then you're spiraling for hours.

That's cortisol—your brain's stress alarm—shutting down your prefrontal cortex *(Arnsten, 2009)*.

So I started using body-first resets:

• Cold face splash

• Chewing ice (or gum in the winter)

• Gripping textured fabric

• Lo-fi beats and coconut

- Dancing in the living room

- Belly breathing: in for 4, hold for 4, out for 8

How it worked for me

I didn't realize how deeply stress was affecting me.

Now, I intervene early.

Not with thinking—

With sensation.

These simple reset rituals don't "solve" anything.

But they interrupt the spiral.

They help me come back to my body, and from there —back to clarity.

Cold water. Soft music. Coconut oil.

I use them like lifelines.

And they work.

TOOL 5: ENERGY-RAMPING MICRO-RITUALS

How it was born

My brain doesn't turn on like a light switch.

It ramps.

And sometimes, it resists entirely.

So I built a playful little toolkit.

Not for productivity.

For permission.

• When I feel the fog, I do 90 seconds of movement

• When I can't start, I change rooms

• When my mind is mush, I play with color, sound, texture

Even novelty is a tool:

• A new pen

• A new playlist

• A new snack

ADHD doesn't respond to "should."

It responds to stimulation.

I stopped waiting for discipline.

I started building interest.

That's the ignition *(Volkow et al., 2009)*.

How it worked for me

I stopped blaming myself for "not starting."

Instead, I gave myself permission to ramp up.

Feeling foggy? I'd stretch in a different room or light a candle.

Needed novelty? I'd grab a new pen, change lighting, or start with a micro-task.

These weren't hacks.

They were invitations.

And they worked.

MEDS: A PERSONALIZED APPROACH

The not-so-ultimate game-changer

I used to be anti-medication. Hardcore.

Tried everything else first: reflexology, Human Design, nutritional hacks.

Anything to avoid a pill.

But ADHD is neurobiological.

You can't just "try harder" and wish it away.

Sometimes, meds are not about numbing—

They're about access (*Shier et al., 2012*).

Here's what I learned:

• *Different brains, different chemistry.*

Some of us thrive on stimulants like methylphenidate or amphetamines—boosting dopamine.

Others prefer non-stimulants like atomoxetine—targeting norepinephrine *(Volkow & Swanson, 2013).*

Nathan and I both take a dopamine-based stimulant that combines different amphetamine salts.

It helps quiet the noise and gives our brains the grip they need.

• *My son Nathan?* Classic hyperactive type. His meds help him sit through a rigid school day.

• *Me?* I'm combined-type. I use meds selectively—on "executive shutdown" days or when I have to do brain-numbing admin.

And sometimes? I skip it.

Some days, I ride the wave without meds.

I let my raw ADHD brilliance lead.

Loud. Tangential. Totally alive.

On those days, I don't need more dopamine—

I am dopamine.

• • •

The point?

Meds aren't a crutch.

They're a key—

When used consciously, respectfully, and with the right support.

For some, they're daily.

For others, they're edge-case days.

No shame. No rules.

Just choice.

TRY THIS IF...

• Coffee is the first thing you consume—and you still feel like a ghost

• Your "healthy eating" habits leave you hangry or crashing

• Your brain spirals after a vague email

• You feel guilty about needing movement before you can "focus"

• You've been blaming yourself for a dopamine deficiency you didn't cause

GENTLE PRACTICE PROMPT

Tomorrow morning, before you check your phone, ask:

"What's one kind thing I can do for my dopamine today?"

Then do it.

No permission required.

WHAT'S NEXT

Now that you've met the chemistry beneath your chaos,

we're heading toward momentum and mastery.

The next chapter is about executive function:

The part of your brain that plans, starts, follows through...

or forgets and spirals.

Chapter 4 is where we stop shaming the shutdown—

And start launching in ways that actually work.

Let's build your momentum system.

Chapter 4

LAUNCH SEQUENCE
INTERRUPTED

WORKING WITH EXECUTIVE
DYSFUNCTION, NOT AGAINST IT

OPENING GROUNDING MOMENT

You know that thing where your brain says, "Let's go!"

and your body says... absolutely nothing?

Yeah. Same.

Executive dysfunction isn't laziness.

It's trying to start a car with no key, no gas, and seven iPhone reminders popping up that all say *"Do the thing."*

This chapter is your ignition reset.

Not with shame.

With strategy. And a wink.

Because starting isn't about being better—

it's about being understood.

WHAT THIS CHAPTER HELPS YOU DO

This chapter helps you move from freeze to flow—

not by forcing productivity,

but by finding your ignition.

You'll build your own micro-launch system,

learn to see time like a living map,

create rescue scripts for the moments logic leaves the building, and turn your chaos into something you can externalize.

Most of all?

You'll learn how to stop starting alone.

Because some of us don't need a better plan—

we need a witness.

Let's rebuild your launchpad.

One spark at a time.

TOOL 1: TWO-MINUTE LAUNCHERS

How it was born

You don't need a full plan.

You need a doorway.

That's what the two-minute rule became for me.

If it takes less than two minutes, I do it now.

And if it's bigger? I just do one part of it.

Open the tab. Write one sentence. Put on the shoes.

That's all. But that's the ignition.

This tool interrupts perfectionism.

It bypasses the panic.

It offers momentum—without expectation.

This is a solo ignition system.

It doesn't require readiness.

Just presence, and a little bravery *(Weigard et al., 2019).*

How it worked for me

I used to stare at tasks like they were Mount Everest —too big to start.

But once I committed to taking the smallest possible action—just two minutes—

it was like I found a hidden door.

For example:

Just write one sentence. That's it.

Suddenly, I wasn't so overwhelmed. I wasn't stuck. I was moving.

I used to wait for the perfect plan, the perfect mood, the perfect window.

But ADHD rarely gives you perfect.

Now I believe this:

Done is better than perfect, especially when perfect keeps you stuck. 80% done is still done. And way better than not started.

Two-minute actions were my way of outsmarting the paralysis.

Not with willpower—just with a window.

TOOL 2: TIME BLINDNESS VISUAL ANCHORS

How it was born

I don't feel time pass.

My body doesn't register it.

So I stopped pretending it did.

I started using visible pacing anchors and labels that speak ADHD fluently.

I break my day into visual zones:

- Before Lunch

- After Walk

- Night Mode

My alarms don't say "Meeting at 2."

They say "Begin Soft Wrap-Up Now."

Because the ADHD brain doesn't just need reminders.

It needs transitions that land like a whisper, not a whip *(Barkley, 1997).*

How it worked for me

Time blindness made it impossible to stay on track.

I'd look up and realize hours had vanished—or that I was late again.

So I stopped relying on abstract time

and started giving it shape.

Big visual anchors. Color-coded blocks.

Alarms with emotional language:

"Wind it down, babe" instead of "YOU'RE LATE."

These weren't reminders.

They were re-entries.

And they grounded me.

TOOL 3: IF-THEN RESCUE SCRIPTS

How it was born

When my brain crashes into a wall, logic goes offline.

I can't problem-solve. I can barely remember what I was trying to do.

So I build rescue scripts ahead of time.

Micro-instructions from my calm self, written for my future scrambled self:

• If I freeze, then I do three slow exhales and reread one past win

• If I spiral into "not good enough," then I grab my grounding stone and name three things I've already done today

• If I forget what I was doing, then I glance at my "Reset the Loop" sticky note

These aren't silly tricks.

They're scaffolding.

Pre-installed safety rails written in the language my brain understands *(Castellanos et al., 2006).*

How it worked for me

When I hit a wall, everything went dim.

My thoughts scrambled. My body froze.

Even breathing felt like a puzzle.

So I turned to the scripts—my personal manual.

"Three breaths. One win."

That one line broke the panic loop.

These didn't fix the freeze.

They gave me something to reach for

when I couldn't think clearly enough to find it myself.

TOOL 4: MEMORY ANCHORS

How it was born

Working memory?

More like disappearing ink.

So I stopped trying to hold everything in my head.

I started speaking aloud like a narrator:

- *"I'm putting the passport in the red folder"*

- *"I've already texted the school"*

- *"I've watered my plant. I've watered my plant."*

I also externalize my thoughts: whiteboards, visual cues, task cards.

It's not ridiculous.

It's required *(Martinussen et al., 2005)*.

How it worked for me

I used to beat myself up for forgetting simple things.

Then I stopped expecting my brain to hold it all.

Instead, I anchored it.

Saying things out loud.

Writing them on sticky notes.

Designating visual zones.

It was like clearing cache.

Less brain clutter. More flow.

Where Tool 3 gives me emotional resets,

this gives me practical cognitive scaffolding—

for everyday working memory.

TOOL 5: THE BODY-DOUBLE BLUEPRINT

How it was born

Sometimes I don't need a better plan.

I need a witness.

A body double isn't a coach.

It's not a babysitter.

And it's definitely not there to guilt-trip you into productivity.

It's just another nervous system breathing in the same room—

so mine remembers what it came here to do.

This is co-regulated ignition.

Here's how I build mine

• The Invite:

"Hey. Want to be my human loading bar?

I've got a thing to do, and I just need someone co-existing while I try to start.

Totally silent is fine—just presence helps."

• Choose Your Mode:

– Silent Parallel Work: camera on, no pressure

– Lo-Fi Accountability Loops: "I opened the file." "I sent the email."

– Timer-Based Sprinting: 25 min on, 5 min break. Shared start, mutual exhale.

• The Exit Ritual:

End with a "we did it."

A thumbs up.

A "damn, we showed up" *(Cleveland Clinic, 2025).*

Because body-doubling isn't about finishing.

It's about not doing it alone.

ADHD is a co-regulation sport.

Sometimes, the spark lives in someone else's steady breath.

How it worked for me

When I finally stopped doing everything solo, my momentum came back.

I asked a friend to be my weekly check-in buddy.

Every Monday, I'd send him a messy writing draft—

and he'd reply with a nudge:

"Hey, have you drifted?"

I had time angels, too—

people who'd call before meetups

to help me peel away from the laptop and remember to live.

Together, they turned chaos into consistency.

And ADHD into something I didn't have to manage alone.

TRY THIS IF...

- Your to-do list makes your brain shut down

- You know what to do but can't seem to start

- You plan perfectly and still panic

- You circle a task for hours and feel shattered

- Your motivation comes alive when someone else is just... there

GENTLE PRACTICE PROMPT

Tonight, pick one small thing that's been haunting you.

Set a timer. Two minutes.

Start. Then stop.

That's all.

You did it.

WHAT'S NEXT

You've built a better launch system.

But what if your ignition misfires once a month—

or once a week—

and you can't explain why?

In **Chapter 5**, we're diving into the hormonal tides that shift your symptoms.

Because your ADHD isn't always the same.

And your tools shouldn't be either.

Chapter 5

HORMONES & THE ADHD BODY

RIDING THE REAL CYCLES
BENEATH THE CRASH

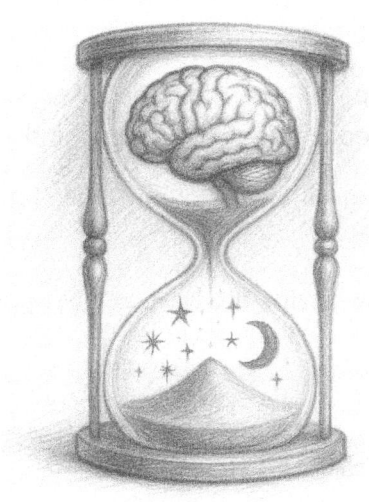

OPENING GROUNDING MOMENT

One week you're a productivity goddess.

The next, you're crying over a cereal commercial and forgetting where you put your soul (and also your keys).

Sound familiar?

This isn't chaos.

This is chemistry.

And no, you're not imagining it.

This chapter isn't here to make your cycle "better."

It's here to help you track your tides like the brilliant, emotional meteorologist of your own mind.

Because syncing with your hormones isn't giving up control—

it's learning how to ride the wave without getting wrecked.

WHAT THIS CHAPTER HELPS YOU DO

This chapter helps you decode your body's internal rhythms—

not as obstacles, but as intel.

You'll learn to track your own patterns,

move your big stuff to power days,

soften on your crash days,

and advocate for your body like the ADHD genius you are.

Because your brain doesn't operate in isolation.

When your hormones shift,

your ADHD shifts too.

Let's build a system that moves with you, not against you.

TOOL 1: CYCLE-AWARE SYMPTOM TRACKER

How it was born

I use a plain paper calendar.

No apps.

Just four colors of highlighter and my body's truth.

• Pink = energy

• Blue = brain fog

• Orange = overwhelm

• Green = grounded

Each day I track just one word.

Over time, a map emerges—

of when my ADHD spikes,

when clarity returns,

and which days hold creative gold.

This isn't about control.

It's about clarity *(Roberts et al., 2018)*.

How it worked for me

I used to feel confused and caught off guard by my fluctuations.

Some days I was unstoppable.

Other days I couldn't move.

Once I started tracking my mood and function in simple color-coded words, everything changed.

I saw where the fog landed.

Where my spark returned.

When I needed softness.

When I could sprint.

This tool didn't fix my cycle.

It gave me visibility—

and the power to plan around it.

TOOL 2: FOLLICULAR VS. LUTEAL PHASE PLANNING

How it was born

Once I had my personal map, I needed to understand the biology behind it.

Estrogen rises in the follicular phase (post-period), which boosts dopamine.

That's when I plan:

- Big projects

- Batch hard conversations

- Pitch ideas

In the luteal phase (pre-period), progesterone takes over.

More emotional intensity. Less executive clarity.

That's when I:

• Avoid high-stakes decision-making

• Build in 15% buffer time

• Use checklists and scripts

• Front-load rest

Working with my cycle doesn't make me less productive.

It makes me sustainable *(Roberts et al., 2017)*.

How it worked for me

Once I started learning the science behind the phases, it all made sense.

I wasn't inconsistent.

I was hormonal.

Instead of pushing through the luteal crash, I gave myself permission to plan differently.

I tackled hard things during my estrogen surge.

I saved repetitive tasks and recovery for my progesterone wave.

This wasn't about fragility.

It was strategy.

And it worked.

TOOL 3: THYROID SYMPTOM CHECK-IN & ADVOCACY SCRIPT

How it was born

If you're constantly foggy, fatigued, or forgetful—

even when you're "doing everything right"—check your thyroid.

I brought this script to my doctor:

"I'm noticing memory problems, extreme fatigue, mood swings, and weight loss that don't match my usual ADHD patterns. I've been having trouble sleeping, I've lost my appetite, and I just feel off. Can we run a full thyroid panel, including T3, T4, and antibodies?"

You're not being dramatic.

You're being thorough *(Grigorova & Sherwin, 2012).*

How it worked for me

I was losing weight without trying.

I couldn't sleep.

My appetite vanished.

Nothing felt familiar—

not even my own mind.

Eventually, I spoke up and asked for the full thyroid panel.

That changed everything.

My numbers were off.

And once I got treatment, my focus returned,

my mood stabilized,

and I stopped thinking I was losing my mind.

Knowing the chemical why brought me back to myself.

TOOL 4: CORTISOL RECOVERY RITUAL

How it was born

You've already met my cortisol rescue toolkit—cold splash, breath, grounding.

This one's for recovery.

A softer ritual.

A letting-go ceremony.

Not for stopping the flood.

For settling after it.

My evening wind-down now looks like this:

- Legs up on the couch

- Weighted pillow on my chest

- Breathe in 4, hold 4, exhale 8

- Whisper: *"You're safe now. You can soften."*

This isn't a vibe.

It's neurobiology.

Letting your nervous system exhale *(Arnsten, 2009)*.

How it worked for me

I used to "go to bed" like it was a light switch.

Spoiler: It wasn't.

I'd lie there, body tense, brain in overdrive.

No off button.

Now I escort myself down.

The pillow. The breath. The whisper.

Not to perform peace—

to offer it.

This ritual doesn't knock me out.

It brings me in.

. . .

TOOL 5: HORMONAL TRANSITION MAP (PUBERTY, PREGNANCY, POSTPARTUM—AND LATER)

How it was born

Puberty made my ADHD louder.

Pregnancy made it clearer.

Postpartum made it vanish—then come back swinging.

Perimenopause?

I'm not there yet,

but I'm not walking into it blind.

Name your phases.

Map how your ADHD showed up in each.

What worked.

What didn't.

This isn't just self-awareness.

It's survival *(Young et al., 2020)*.

How it worked for me

Every hormonal season reshaped my ADHD.

Puberty? Chaos.

Pregnancy? Clarity.

Postpartum? Disappearance—then a crash.

I didn't understand it until I wrote it down.

I tracked the flavors of my brain across each transition.

What helped.

What harmed.

What saved me.

This map became my guide.

And I'm making room on it—for what's next.

TRY THIS IF...

• Your brain feels like a different person every week

• You keep planning like a robot and crashing like a human

• You cry during commercials and then shame spiral about it

• Your focus vanishes the week before your period

• Your doctor said "that's just hormones" and sent you home

GENTLE PRACTICE PROMPT

What if your "mood swings" were actually moon swings?

What if your chemistry wasn't the problem—

but the compass?

WHAT'S NEXT

Now that you've met your cycles, let's meet your senses.

Because the next crash?

It doesn't come from hormones.

It comes from emotional waves, buzzing lights, itchy shirts, and the shame that clings to *"too much."*

Next up: **Chapter 6** — Emotional Thunder & Sensory Storms.

Let's go soften the storm—

without shutting yourself down.

Chapter 6

EMOTIONAL THUNDER & SENSORY STORMS

REGULATING WITHOUT LOSING THE MAGIC

OPENING GROUNDING MOMENT

There's that moment.

You're totally fine... until you're absolutely not.

A comment hits wrong.

A light flickers too loud.

A tag in your shirt feels like betrayal.

And suddenly, you're unraveling.

This isn't "dramatic."

This is data.

If your emotions feel like tidal waves

and your senses hijack your day—welcome.

You're not broken.

You're brilliantly tuned.

This chapter doesn't ask you to toughen up.

It invites you to soften into understanding.

We're not dimming your magic.

We're helping you hold it.

WHAT THIS CHAPTER HELPS YOU DO

This chapter helps you ride emotional waves without drowning—

and regulate your senses without disappearing.

You'll learn how to name what's happening,

listen to your nervous system,

and map the people, places, and practices that help you feel safe.

You'll track the cost of masking,

rewrite the rejection loop,

and reclaim your sensitivity as the superpower it's always been.

Because when you stop fighting the storm,

you don't just survive it.

You learn how to live inside it—on your terms.

TOOL 1: DBT-STYLE EMOTION RIDING

How it was born

Urge surfing. Opposite action. Emotion naming.

They sound clinical, maybe even cold—

but they're not.

They're lifelines for ADHDers who feel everything at Level 100.

They come from Dialectical Behavior Therapy—DBT for short.

Built for big feelings. For stormy minds.

Crafted by psychologist Marsha Linehan, DBT was designed to help people ride emotional waves without drowning *(Linehan, 1993)*.

Turns out, it's not just for crisis.

It's for *us*, too.

I started saying my emotions out loud—even the ugly ones:

"This is panic." "This is rage." "This is grief."

Naming them like old friends stopped the spiral

before it could tighten.

And opposite action? That was gold.

When I wanted to crawl into a dark room and shut everyone out,

I'd open the blinds.

Light wasn't a cure.

But it reminded me I was still here. Still in charge.

How it worked for me

At first, naming what I felt was impossible.

A comment would detonate me. I'd spiral fast.

But saying *"This is panic"* out loud gave me distance.

It created space to breathe.

Opposite action helped too.

When I wanted to disappear,

I did the smallest thing that moved me toward the world.

Open the blinds. Step outside. Stretch.

That shift—tiny but conscious—was enough to turn the tide.

TOOL 2: SENSORY KIT BUILDER

How it was born

I keep a sensory kit in every zone of my life—purse, car, desk drawer.

For some, it's fidgets. For others, soft textures.

For me? AirPods. Sunglasses. Chloe perfume.

A weighted hoodie I call *"my armor."*

Polyvagal Theory helped me understand something big:

when your nervous system feels safe, your brain can start to regulate again.

So I stopped treating my senses like optional extras—

and started honoring them as sacred inputs *(Porges, 2007).*

How it worked for me

I used to push through sensory overload.

Loud rooms. Harsh lights. Tight clothes.

And then wondered why I melted down.

Once I created my kits—

AirPods for sound, sunglasses for glare, hoodie for comfort—

I had a portable reset button.

These weren't indulgences.

They were protection.

And they worked.

TOOL 3: SENSORY SAFE ZONES MAP

How it was born

While my kits go with me, this tool is about the spaces that already hold me.

Your nervous system has favorite corners—

it just hasn't been asked where they are.

So I started mapping mine:

- The garden chair where I feel grounded
- The couch corner with the softest light
- The room I avoid because it buzzes too loud

I made a sketch—color-coded for calm, overstim, and *"just right."*

Now I know where to go

when my brain hits red alert.

Because sometimes, it's not about adding tools.

It's about claiming the ones already around you
(Clément et al., 2022).

How it worked for me

I didn't realize my overwhelm was environmental.

But once I mapped my spaces,

I saw how much my nervous system already knew.

I started using the garden chair when I needed peace.

The soft-lit corner for focus.

Avoiding rooms that felt "loud," even in silence.

These zones became anchors.

Places to come back to myself—without explanation.

TOOL 4: MASKING FATIGUE TRACKER

How it was born

We started this in Chapter 2. This is the evolution.

Not just when I masked—

but what it cost me.

- When did I pretend?

- When did I shrink?

- When did I vanish?

Masking may look like:

- Nodding when confused

- Saying yes with resentment

- Rehearsing texts over and over

- Holding in stims or tears

- Smiling when you feel like screaming

The first step to healing was naming.

Masking isn't weakness.

It's exhaustion.

It's self-abandonment on repeat.

And eventually, the interest comes due.

And unmasking—slowly, safely—is power reclaimed.

Especially for women and girls, who so often carry the silent weight of "just try harder" on their backs.

Research shows that girls with ADHD are often under-identified and more likely to internalize—

shrinking smaller, trying harder to hide.

We smile more. We say less. We shape-shift to survive *(Slobodin & Davidovitch, 2019).*

No wonder we're tired. No wonder we vanish.

How it worked for me

I didn't know how much of me I was hiding

until I started naming it.

I saw where I bent myself to fit.

Where I over-smiled.

Where I edited my intensity down to "acceptable."

Tracking this gave me something I didn't expect: permission.

Permission to step back.

To take off the mask.

To speak like myself again.

Even when it felt raw, it felt real.

And that was the beginning of coming home.

TOOL 5: RSD REALITY-CHECK JOURNAL

How it was born

When that rejection storm hits,

I journal the story I'm telling myself.

Then I write at least three alternate stories.

"She ignored me" becomes:

- "Maybe she's tired."

- "Maybe she's scared."

- "Maybe I'm projecting."

Rejection Sensitivity isn't made up. It's not a character flaw.

It's studied. Documented. Real.

In ADHD brains—especially young ones—justice

wounds cut deep, and a "no" can feel like an earthquake.

The science says it's not in your head. It's in your wiring *(Bondü & Esser, 2015)*.

But now you get to choose how you ride the wave.

Your stories aren't just spirals. They're signals. And you can rewrite them.

How it worked for me

Rejection used to flatten me.

One comment. One pause. One look—

and I'd crumble.

Then I started writing.

One story. Three possibilities.

"Maybe they didn't see the message."

"Maybe they're overwhelmed."

"Maybe this has nothing to do with me."

It didn't erase the sting.

But it gave me a bridge.

Something to walk myself across

when shame tried to swallow me whole.

RSD isn't weakness.

It's unmet sensitivity.

And you can meet it now.

And some mornings?

I still look in the mirror, hand on my heart, and whisper,

"Hey, little me. You're safe now. I've got you."

I say it out loud—so my nervous system hears it too.

When I feel myself spiraling?

I name three things I'm grateful for.

Even the small stuff—

clean socks, sunlight on tile,

the exact right cup of tea.

Gratitude softens the edge of emotional freefall.

It reminds me I'm still here. Still held.

TRY THIS IF...

• You cry "too easily" and have been shamed for it your whole life

• You shut down from loud noises, bright lights, or scratchy clothes

• You feel exhausted after socializing—even with people you love

• You've rewritten the same text message seventeen times

• You're starting to realize your "intensity" is a gift—not a glitch

• You want to feel more grounded, but don't know where to start

And if all else fails? Try this:

Name three things you're grateful for.

Right now.

Even if they're tiny.

Even if it feels silly.

Gratitude can't erase the storm,

but it can hold your hand through it.

GENTLE PRACTICE PROMPT

Tonight, place your hand on your chest and whisper:

"My emotions are allowed. My sensitivity is sacred. My brain is not a battle—I am home here."

And if you need an anchor in the morning, just say:

"I've got you now, little one. We're safe."

Because healing doesn't always roar.

Sometimes, it whispers.

And sometimes, that's enough.

WHAT'S NEXT

You've anchored your sensitivity and honored your emotions.

Now we shift from the internal tides...

to the external terrain.

In **Chapter 7**, we'll dive into your real-life chaos—

clutter piles, impulse scrolls, half-finished lists.

We're not going to tidy up your brain.

We're going to build systems that actually work for it.

Chapter 7

FUNCTIONING IN
THE MESS

RHYTHMS, NOT RULES. SUPPORT,
NOT SHAME

CHAPTER 7: FUNCTIONING IN THE MESS

BUILDING SYSTEMS THAT ACTUALLY WORK FOR YOUR ADHD BRAIN

OPENING GROUNDING MOMENT

Forget the brain scans and research papers—

this is where ADHD shows up in your fridge.

In your unopened mail.

In that weird corner of your living room where half your to-dos go to die.

This is the chapter where we get real about what it means to function

when your executive system is running on whim, vibe,

and whatever playlist happens to be working today.

This is where you stop trying to live like a productivity Pinterest board—

and start building systems that respect your reality.

WHAT THIS CHAPTER HELPS YOU DO

This chapter gives you everyday tools that meet you in the middle of the mess.

You'll learn how to pause the dopamine scroll,

work with your clutter (not against it),

reconnect after ghosting,

track burnout before it crashes you,

and separate your worth from your output.

This isn't about tidying up your life.

It's about building rituals that respect your brain's real, raw rhythm.

No shame.

No sparkle filters.

Just support that fits your frequency.

TOOL 1: THE IMPULSE PAUSE PROTOCOL

How it was born

Impulse spending was my toxic ex.

Emotional stress? Buy a book.

Low dopamine? Buy 12 lipsticks.

ADHD brains are wired for phasic dopamine—fast, spiky hits *(Del Campo et al., 2011).*

The trick isn't shame. It's pause.

Here's what I do now:

• When the urge hits, I whisper: *"This is a dopamine decision."*

• I screenshot the item. Not buy—just screenshot.

• I wait 24 hours. Sometimes 48. Then check: still want it?

• Bonus: I have a folder called *"Could Have Bought"*

→ Looking at it gives me dopamine too.

You're not impulsive because you're weak.

You're impulsive because your reward system is starving.

Feed it differently. Feed it slowly.

That's power.

· · ·

How it worked for me

Impulse buying was a cycle I couldn't break—

until I stopped trying to break it,

and started rerouting it.

Screenshots instead of checkouts.

Delays instead of denial.

It wasn't about punishing my brain.

It was about giving it something better.

TOOL 2: THE ONE-TOUCH RULE (HOME EDITION)

How it was born

Clutter loops were killing my spoons.

Dishes piled up.

Mail multiplied.

Socks formed their own civil society.

Executive dysfunction + working memory issues = tornado house *(Willcutt et al., 2005)*.

Now? If I touch something, I resolve it.

• Dirty dish? Into the dishwasher.

• Opened mail? Deal with it or drop it in the *Action Tray*.

- Coat on chair? Gets hung up.

If I can't do it fully, I drop it in a visible *LATER* bin—

and I schedule that bin on my calendar.

You've met its cousin—the two-minute launcher.

This is the home version.

Same heartbeat. Different room.

This is about external structure, not internal urge.

It's how I build rhythm into my space.

How it worked for me

Before this rule, clutter was constant static.

Now, it's a rhythm I can hear.

One object. One choice.

Not all of it—just one thing at a time.

I didn't need a spotless house.

I needed a supportive one.

TOOL 3: THE SOCIAL REPAIR TEMPLATE

How it was born

I've ghosted people I love.

Not because I didn't care—

but because my executive function collapsed under the pressure of replying "right."

ADHDers often struggle with social timing, tone tracking, and follow-up *(Capuozzo et al., 2024).*

So now, I keep a message saved in my notes:

"Hey love, I disappeared and it wasn't because I don't care.

My ADHD got loud. I spiraled.

And now I'm coming back with awkwardness and love.

No pressure. Just a hug if you want it."

90% of the time? People get it.

10%? They weren't safe for my real self anyway.

This isn't about explaining perfectly.

It's about reconnecting without shame.

How it worked for me

The guilt spiral of ghosting used to keep me away longer.

This message helped me return—awkward, yes, but honest.

It removed the script pressure.

It let me come back with softness instead of shame.

And if someone couldn't hold that?

They weren't mine to hold anyway.

TOOL 4: THE BURNOUT BAROMETER

How it was born

This isn't about clutter.

This is about energy collapse.

Burnout doesn't announce itself.

It creeps. Slowly. Quietly.

So I built a barometer to catch the creep:

• When was the last time I said no?

• Am I using caffeine to survive?

• Have I skipped joy for more than 3 days?

• Does everything feel urgent?

If I tick more than 2 boxes, I switch into Minimum Viable Day mode:

• Eat something

• Move a little

- One human interaction (even a barista counts)

- Stop working after 6 p.m.

This isn't laziness.

It's preventative medicine *(Surman et al., 2013).*

How it worked for me

I used to think burnout was a crash.

It's not. It's a leak.

Tracking those quiet leaks saved me.

Minimum Viable Days became a way to reset

before I broke down.

I still get tired.

But I don't disappear anymore.

TOOL 5: THE SELF-WORTH LOG

How it was born

I used to only feel valuable when I was checking boxes.

Twelve tasks a day or I was failing.

Now I end each night with this prompt:

"Today I showed up by..."

- texting a friend back

- hugging Nathan when he needed it

- not quitting on myself

Then I write:

"I mattered today because I EXISTED."

This isn't productivity.

This is proof.

Some nights, I sketch a little heart beside it.

Art becomes my affirmation.

I collage my worth with color, not checklists.

I don't earn rest anymore.

I just claim it—because I'm alive.

(Ginapp et al., 2023) shows we're not deficient—we're dysregulated.

And regulation comes through recognizing our value, not measuring it.

How it worked for me

I used to think I had to earn rest.

Now I know I deserve it because I'm human.

This practice helps me close the day gently.

No matter how messy it was.

It reminds me that existence is enough.

And small acts of care are radical.

Some nights I still write it like a mantra:

"I am worthy. I am enough. I choose kindness toward myself today."

TRY THIS IF...

- You've bought three planners and still feel lost

- You keep ghosting people and then spiral in shame

- You open your fridge and feel deep existential dread

- You're carrying guilt for "not doing enough" again

- You feel like your house reflects your failure (it doesn't)

GENTLE PRACTICE PROMPT

Write this on a sticky note:

"My system doesn't have to be pretty. It has to be mine."

Stick it where your judgment usually lives.

Also try this:

Stand in front of a mirror.

Place your hand on your heart.

Whisper: *"I was always enough."*

Let it land.

WHAT'S NEXT

You've mapped the mess.

You've built tools that hold you—not scold you.

Now we follow the spiral down into the quiet part of the loop—

where sleep never comes on time, dopamine gets borrowed from tomorrow,

and your brain throws its own afterparty.

In **Chapter 8**, we'll meet your crash cycles and late-night scrolls with compassion—

and build real rest into your rhythm.

Chapter 8

SLEEP, SUBSTANCES & SELF-MEDICATION

REGULATING WITHOUT THE
CRASH-CYCLE SPIRAL

OPENING GROUNDING MOMENT

Let's be real: you've tried everything.

Magnesium. Meditation.

Journaling by candlelight while whispering
affirmations

and pretending you're not already spiraling into a
YouTube hole

about *"how to fix sleep naturally."*

This chapter isn't here to judge you

for doomscrolling at 2:44 a.m.

It's here to sit beside you,

whisper *"me too,"*

and hand you a better plan—

one that starts with understanding, not guilt.

Because rest? For ADHD brains?

It's not just bedtime—

it's a full-body rebellion against the world's noise.

Let's make peace with the night.

WHAT THIS CHAPTER HELPS YOU DO

This chapter helps you untangle your nighttime rituals

from your coping mechanisms.

You'll stop mistaking stimulation for connection,

and silence for failure.

You'll build gentle wind-downs,

swap emergency dopamine fixes for sustainable rituals,

and learn how to meet your wired brain without shaming it.

Rest isn't something you earn—

it's something you relearn.

This is where we start.

TOOL 1: MELATONIN—MY TINY BUT MIGHTY RESET BUTTON

How it was born

The ADHD brain often releases melatonin late—like, really late.

Which is why *"just go to bed earlier"* is both hilarious and impossible.

What actually helps? A micro-dose.

I take 0.5 mg between 6:30–7:00 p.m., when I'm trying to nudge my rhythm gently toward earlier sleep *(van Andel et al., 2021).*

Not to knock me out—just to give my brain the memo: bedtime's on the way.

How it worked for me

Sleep wasn't the problem. It was the start and stop.

My brain never signaled, *"Hey, wind down."*

It just kept going.

Melatonin didn't knock me out—

It signaled the shift. It became the cue: *we're moving from go to slow.*

A tiny ritual. A gentle reset.

Not a fix. But a flag in the ground.

. . .

TOOL 2: BRIGHT LIGHT AS A BRAIN-ANCHOR

How it was born

Where Tool 1 helped me wind down, this one helps my body wake up—on purpose.

I used to scroll first thing in the morning.

Until I learned that 10,000 lux of bright light within the first hour of waking can shift your whole biological clock *(Fargason et al., 2017)*.

So now?

- I open the curtains

- I take a cold shower

- I move around a bit

- I sit on my patio with my coffee

That morning light? It anchors me in time.

It starts the sleep cycle—just twelve hours ahead.

How it worked for me

Reaching for my phone first thing only made the overwhelm worse.

Bright light, movement, cold—those became my new inputs.

And they shifted my entire rhythm.

It wasn't just feeling better.

It was telling my body what time it is.

TOOL 3: MY 20-MINUTE POWER RESET

How it was born

When I've been in hyperfocus or Zoom fatigue, my brain hits a wall.

I used to reach for sugar.

Now? I lie down.

No pressure to nap—just rest.

Eyes closed. Brown noise. Twenty minutes.

Even when I don't sleep, it works.

My nervous system gets the message: *you're safe to reboot (Sobanski et al., 2008).*

How it worked for me

I used to treat tiredness like something to push through.

But it wasn't weakness—it was overload.

This reset wasn't about doing more later.

It was about not unraveling now.

326

Twenty minutes. No demands.

Just a nervous system asking for pause—

and finally getting it.

TOOL 4: THE DOPAMINE REPLACEMENT PLAN

How it was born

You've already seen how I use food as fuel back in Chapter 3.

But late at night? I'm not fueling. I'm coping.

This plan isn't about nutrients.

It's about swapping dopamine-on-credit for something sustainable.

This is my after-dark dopamine menu—less about fueling, more about soothing.

Before, I'd reach for:

• Sugar

• Caffeine

• TikTok scroll loops

Now I've built gentler swaps:

• Instead of milk chocolate → protein + crunch (cashews, carrots)

• Instead of another latte → water, peppermint oil, or a walk

• Instead of scrolling → write my ideas, listen to a book, play lo-fi

Not every choice is perfect.

But enough swaps = a new cycle *(Del Campo et al., 2011).*

How it worked for me

That late-night *"I need something"* feeling?

It wasn't always hunger. It was dopamine.

Once I swapped in soothing alternatives—protein, movement, silence—

I didn't just feel better.

I felt stable.

Not a crash. Not a sprint.

Just... okay.

And sometimes? That's the win.

TOOL 5: MY SENSORY WIND-DOWN MENU

How it was born

You've met my sensory kit before—AirPods, textures, noise loops.

This is its nighttime sibling.

Not for daytime regulation—

for slowing the spin,

softening the spark,

and opening the door to sleep.

My current wind-down mix:

- Warm shower

- Cozy slippers

- Herbal tea

- Weighted blanket

- One non-stimulating chapter from a book

- Lo-fi beats or rain sounds

It doesn't calm me down.

It signals that *we're done*.

That's not a checklist.

It's a nervous system love note *(Coogan & McGowan, 2017)*.

· · ·

How it worked for me

I used to think I had to flip a switch.

Turn off the chaos. Silence myself into sleep.

Didn't work.

This ritual gave me something to walk into.

A sequence that soothed me.

Warm water. Soft light. Familiar rhythm.

Even when my brain was wired, the message was clear:

We're done for the day. It's safe to soften now.

TRY THIS IF...

• You're a night owl and can't explain why you suddenly feel "alive" at midnight

• Your coffee habit has become a personality trait

• Your brain's version of a bedtime story is replaying every awkward moment from age 7

• Your *"just one scroll"* turns into a three-hour TikTok marathon

• You've ever used sugar, noise, or chaos just to feel something

GENTLE PRACTICE PROMPT

Tonight, instead of pushing through your second wind, ask:

"What would it feel like to let my body lead this time?"

Then give yourself one small signal:

soft socks, a dark room, silence.

Let sleep come when it's ready—

but open the door.

WHAT'S NEXT

You've softened your rhythm and built rituals for real rest.

Now we zoom out—

wider than bedtime.

Deeper than dopamine.

Because sometimes it's not just ADHD.

It's trauma. Anxiety. Burnout. Perfectionism.

The survival system beneath the surface.

In **Chapter 9**, we'll explore your full neurodivergent constellation—

and build tools that hold *all* your layers.

Chapter 9

ADHD & THE REST OF THE BRAIN PARTY

CO-EXISTING CONDITIONS,
COMPASSIONATE CLARITY

OPENING GROUNDING MOMENT

Ever feel like you're doing *"all the right things"* for your ADHD and still... something's off?

Like the fog won't lift.

The panic doesn't quit.

The spiral feels deeper than distraction.

Yeah. Same.

This chapter isn't here to hand you another label.

It's here to finally say:

If your ADHD feels like it brought friends—

anxiety, depression, trauma, perfectionism—

you're not defeated.

You're layered.

We're not fragmenting you.

We're meeting all your pieces.

With curiosity.

With care.

With full permission to support your whole self.

WHAT THIS CHAPTER HELPS YOU DO

This chapter helps you zoom out.

To stop blaming yourself when a tool stops working.

To start asking better questions like,

"What else is happening in my system?"

You'll learn to recognize overlap,

build gentler scaffolding,

and stop gaslighting yourself when healing takes more than one strategy.

This is where we stop trying to fit into boxes—

and start naming every brilliant, bruised, and beautiful part

of your neurodivergent mind.

TOOL 1: THE WHOLE-BRAIN REFLECTION MAP

How it was born

I used to think if I could just get my ADHD *"under control,"* everything else would fall into place.

But what if the everything else was part of the picture all along?

Now, when a tool stops working or I feel emotionally out of sync, I pause and ask:

- Is this executive dysfunction?

- Is this lack of dopamine?

- Is this RSD?

- Is this anxiety?

- Is this trauma brain?

- Is this burnout?

- Is this sensory overload?

This simple check-in helped me stop spiraling into *"what's wrong with me?"* and start seeing my full neural context.

Coexisting conditions aren't failure—they're just part of the wiring *(D'Agati et al., 2019).*

How it worked for me

I used to blame myself when things weren't going well.

If I had a bad day, it was easy to fall into the *"I'm failing"* spiral.

But once I started mapping out all the layers—ADHD, anxiety, trauma, burnout—

I realized that everything was connected.

It wasn't just one thing making me struggle.

It was the intersection of my wiring and my environment.

By naming it all, I gave myself permission to stop apologizing for needing extra support.

It became about seeing my full self, rather than beating myself up for every misstep.

TOOL 2: TRAUMA-INFORMED SAFETY RITUAL

How it was born

I used to think trauma had to be *"big."*

But micro-traumas—being constantly misunderstood, shamed, or overstimulated—built a chronic sense of unsafety in my body.

So now I build in safety rituals.

Mine?

- Sitting on my comfy sofa with a soft blanket

- Low lighting

- A coconut-scented candle

- A whispered script: *"This is not that moment. You are safe. You are here."*

- And sometimes, watching Nathan play Fortnite (*he's really good*)

When I feel my chest tighten or my body go numb, I step into that ritual.

It brings me back. Every time *(Stein et al., 2013).*

How it worked for me

There was a time when I didn't realize how deeply unsafe I felt.

It was subtle—just the quiet hum of overstimulation, the stress of feeling constantly *"too much."*

When I discovered that I could reclaim my safety, things started shifting.

The rituals gave me an anchor—

a way to pause and say, *"I'm here now. I'm safe."*

And through that, I could reconnect with myself and move forward.

. . .

TOOL 3: THE LOOP-BREAKER FOR OCD & PERFECTIONISM

How it was born

You've heard me whisper *"This version is allowed"* in earlier chapters.

This one's louder—it's for the perfectionism panic attack.

When ADHD and OCD dance together, this is my way out.

ADHD makes me messy. OCD makes me panic over the mess.

Together, they make me freeze.

When I'm spiraling between *"I have to do it perfectly"* and *"I can't do it at all,"* I break the loop.

• I touch an object—a grounding stone or a pen

• I say: *"This is done for now."*

• Sometimes I write that on a sticky note and slap it on the fridge

It's not about never checking again.

It's about telling your nervous system: *"You're allowed to stop" (Abramovitch et al., 2015).*

. . .

How it worked for me

Perfectionism and ADHD were like a bad dance partner—always pulling me in opposite directions.

On one hand, I was overwhelmed by the chaos.

On the other, I obsessed over the smallest details.

It wasn't until I started breaking that loop—touching something, saying *"done for now"*—that I learned to step out.

It was like saying, *"Okay, I'm allowed to move on even if it's not perfect."*

It was freeing.

TOOL 4: FOOD FEELINGS TRACKER

How it was born

I used to think I had *"no willpower"* around snacks.

But what I really had was an emotional regulation gap.

Now I track how I feel before I eat—not what I eat, just what I'm feeling.

- Am I bored?

- Anxious?

- Tired?

Then I ask:

- Am I eating to fuel or to numb?

- What would help me regulate besides food?

Sometimes the answer is still the chocolate.

But now, it's a choice—not a coping loop *(Levin & Rawana, 2016).*

How it worked for me

Food was my go-to coping mechanism.

But it wasn't always about hunger.

It was about trying to feel better when my emotions were running wild.

When I started checking in—asking if I was eating to numb or to nourish—

I realized I had more power than I thought.

Sometimes I still chose the snack.

But now it was a conscious decision, not an automatic spiral.

TOOL 5: THE SELF-ADVOCACY STARTER PAGE

How it was born

I used to dread doctor's appointments. Or school meetings.

Any moment where I had to explain Nathan's brain— or mine.

Now? I bring a page. Just one. With:

• Diagnosis

• What actually helps (visuals, breaks, check-ins)

• What we need (accommodations, clarity, kindness)

• A line that says:

"This isn't about special treatment. This is about access."

You don't have to overexplain.

You get to ask for support like it's normal—because it is.

Inclusive systems don't wait for breakdowns.

They're built to offer clarity, safety, and support up front *(Russell et al., 2021)*.

How it worked for me

I used to think I had to prove our needs—make a case for our brains.

But a one-page starter changed that.

Clear. Respectful. Direct.

No panic-prep. No over-apology.

Just clarity.

BONUS: DOCTOR TALK SCRIPTS

If you suspect ADHD and anxiety

"Hi, I relate to ADHD symptoms, but I also notice intense worry, overthinking, and panic. I'm not sure which is which—and I'd love your help untangling it without assuming it's just one thing."

If you feel like "too much is overlapping"

"I'm noticing patterns that feel like ADHD, but also trauma, perfectionism, or burnout. Can we explore how these might overlap and not cancel each other out?"

If you need to advocate for your child (or yourself)

"This is not about excuses. This is about access. These are the supports that work. And this is what happens without them."

NEUROPLASTICITY: REWIRING YOUR ADHD BRAIN

Some shifts don't come from plans.

They come from that quiet, holy moment when you say—

"I'm tired of living in my own war zone."

This isn't about pushing harder.

This is about healing smarter.

Unlearning what never belonged.

Reclaiming what's always been yours.

Your ADHD brain isn't broken.

It's just wired for storms—and wild resilience.

And guess what?

It's also wired for change.

CBT: THOUGHT WORK THAT ACTUALLY WORKS

Cognitive Behavioral Therapy cracked open the part of me that believed I was forever *"too much."*

CBT didn't ask me to be positive.

It asked me to be honest.

To challenge the cruel narratives that had been running my mind for decades:

"I'm behind." → *"I move at my own rhythm, and that rhythm is still worthy."*

"I always mess this up." → *"I've messed up before—and still found my way forward."*

CBT helped me install new scripts.

Not fluff. Not denial.

Just better truth *(Lopez et al., 2018).*

TRY THIS IF...

• You've tried every ADHD planner on earth, but still spiral when shame takes the wheel

• You keep asking, "Why do I still feel broken—even when I'm doing everything 'right'?"

• You're navigating anxiety, perfectionism, trauma— and it's all tangled

• You long to feel safe in your own brain, your own body

• You want something deeper than hacks—you want healing that actually rewires

GENTLE PRACTICE PROMPT

Write this in your notes, your journal, or even on your mirror:

"I am not a mess. I am multilingual.

My brain speaks many languages.

I will listen to all of them."

WHAT'S NEXT

You've met your full wiring—

every overlay, every shade,

every *"maybe it's more than ADHD."*

Now it's time to clear the noise.

In **Chapter 10**, we'll confront the myths and shame stories you were handed—

so you can finally stop defending your truth...

and start living it.

Chapter 10

ADHD IS REAL

BURNING THE MYTHS SO WE CAN
BREATHE AGAIN

OPENING GROUNDING MOMENT

Let's be honest—some days, living with ADHD feels less like a diagnosis

and more like a debate.

The side-eyes.

The *"but you're so smart."*

The *"everyone's a little ADHD."*

It's exhausting.

But this chapter?

It's not a debate.

It's a declaration.

You don't have to justify your brain.

You don't have to translate your experience into someone else's language.

This is where we stop arguing

and start rooting into truth—

loud, unshakable, soul-deep truth.

ADHD is real.

And so are you.

WHAT THIS CHAPTER HELPS YOU DO

This chapter helps you let go of the mental gymnastics.

It gives you the language to shut down myths—

internally and externally—without draining your soul.

You'll build scripts, boundaries, and inner shields to protect your energy.

And most importantly?

You'll stop proving yourself,

and start backing yourself.

Not with rage.

With power.

TOOL 1: FACT-BASED MYTH-BUSTER SCRIPTS

How it was born

When someone says, *"Isn't everyone a little ADHD?"* it hits like a punch to the gut.

So I created my own response scripts.

Not to educate everyone.

To protect myself.

Here's what I say now:

"Actually, about 2.58% of adults meet criteria for persistent ADHD—meaning their symptoms began in childhood and continued into adulthood."

"It's not laziness—it's executive dysfunction. My brain's ignition system doesn't fire like yours."

"Girls don't go undiagnosed because they don't have symptoms. They go undiagnosed because they mask them."

These are my scripts.

You can borrow them.

Or write your own.

Trust me: truth said aloud is a form of healing.

How it worked for me

I used to drown in the silence of having to justify my brain.

When someone said, *"Isn't everyone a little ADHD?"* it felt like I had to defend my entire existence.

But when I finally stopped over-explaining and started speaking facts?

Something changed.

I no longer had to beg for validation.

I started protecting my boundaries, sharing the truth without apology, and feeling stronger each time.

TOOL 2: THE INTERNALIZED SHAME DECODER

How it was born

Some lies don't come from others.

They come from inside.

From the old teachers.

The critical parent.

The coworker who rolled their eyes.

The wellness guru who said, *"Just build a routine."*

Here's how I spot the shame loop:

- I hear myself say, *"I should've known better."*

- I pause and ask, *"Whose voice is that?"*

- I whisper, *"That's not mine. That was given to me."*

- I choose a new one: *"I didn't fail. I wasn't supported."*

I don't do this perfectly.

But every time I name the shame and hand it back to its source?

I feel more like myself *(Beaton et al., 2022).*

How it worked for me

For years, I lived under the shadow of shame.

I thought every struggle was my fault—especially when I couldn't meet other people's expectations.

But once I started recognizing those voices that weren't mine, I started reclaiming my own narrative.

Every time I quieted the old, toxic messages and replaced them with something kinder,

I could feel the weight lifting.

I wasn't broken.

I was just operating with different wiring.

TOOL 3: EMOTIONAL SELF-ADVOCACY SCRIPTING

How it was born

Here's the truth: sometimes I still shrink.

In the doctor's office, when they suggest I'm *"just stressed."*

At school meetings, when they talk about Nathan like he's a problem to solve.

At dinner parties, when someone says, *"You're so energetic, you're probably ADHD haha."*

I used to laugh along.

Now? I take a breath and say:

- *"ADHD is real. And it's not a punchline."*

- *"My son's brain isn't flawed. It just works differently."*

- *"I'm not overreacting—I'm setting a boundary"* (Turgay et al., 2012).

I don't need their validation to own my truth.

Neither do you.

How it worked for me

There was a time when I felt like I had to apologize for myself at every turn.

I laughed off ADHD jokes.

Dismissed my struggles.

Hid behind a mask of *"I'm fine."*

But now, when people make light of ADHD, I stand my ground.

I speak with conviction, even if my voice shakes.

Because I know my truth.

And I no longer let others diminish my reality.

TOOL 4: ENERGY-PROTECTION BOUNDARY PLAN

How it was born

You don't have to explain yourself every time someone questions your brain.

Some days, you won't have the energy to *"educate."*

That's okay.

Here's my boundary menu:

- *"This isn't a teaching moment, but here's a resource if you're curious."*

- *"Thanks for your input, but I trust my lived experience."*

- Walk away.

- Log off.

- Unfollow.

- Mute.

You're allowed.

My capacity is finite.

So I guard it like gold *(Quinn & Madhoo, 2014)*.

How it worked for me

I used to be exhausted by the constant need to explain myself—

to friends, doctors, even family.

It wasn't that they didn't care.

It was that they didn't get it.

So I started using boundaries as self-care.

I didn't owe anyone an explanation if I wasn't up for it.

I learned to say no to emotional labor that drained me—

and protect my energy for what truly mattered.

It was empowering.

TOOL 5: COMMUNITY BUILDING START PACK

How it was born

The best thing I ever did for my ADHD?

Find other brains like mine.

Messy. Brilliant. Emotional. Wild. Sacred.

Here's how to start:

• Text a friend: *"Hey. Want to be my body-double on Thursdays?"*

• Join a local ADHD support group. Or start one.

• Host a *Neurodivergent Dinner*—phones off, judgment off, stims welcome.

• Follow one creator who makes your brain feel safe.

Research shows that nonpharmacological strategies—especially when grounded in connection and structure—can make a meaningful difference for ADHD brains *(Sonuga-Barke et al., 2013)*.

And lived experience tells us what the data can't always measure: connection heals.

How it worked for me

After years of feeling like an outsider, I found a tribe that understood me.

People who didn't need me to explain myself.

Who didn't judge my quirks.

Who saw the value in my *"mess."*

Building that community didn't just help me feel
seen—

it helped me feel safe.

The more I surrounded myself with neurodivergent
people,

the more I realized I wasn't *too much*.

I was simply me.

And that was more than enough.

TRY THIS IF...

• You've tried ADHD tools and they work... until they don't

• You're navigating trauma and wondering why you still can't regulate

• You feel like you're *"too sensitive,"* but your gut says otherwise

• You ghost people and wonder if it's social anxiety, not just time blindness

• You feel like there's more going on—but you don't want another label

GENTLE PRACTICE PROMPT

Write this on a sticky note.

Put it where the shame usually speaks:

"I am not a mess. I am multilingual.

My brain speaks many languages.

I will listen to all of them."

WHAT'S NEXT

You've met your full wiring—

every overlay, every shade,

every *"maybe it's more than ADHD."*

Now it's time to clear the static.

Not to erase your story—

but to untangle it from the myths, shame, and masks you were handed.

In **Chapter 11**, we'll dismantle what never belonged to you—

so you can stop defending your truth...

and finally start living it.

Chapter 11

THE ADHD SUPERPOWER SUITE

TURNING YOUR FIRE INTO FOCUS, LEADERSHIP & JOY

OPENING GROUNDING MOMENT

Okay. Deep breath.

You've made it through the myths,

the meltdowns,

the mess.

You've mapped your flavor.

Built your tools.

Untangled the shame spiral.

Now?

We get to talk about the part they never warned you about—

your superpowers.

Yes, you heard me.

The hyperfocus.

The intuitive hits.

The boldness, the humor, the wild creativity

that flips a room on its head.

This isn't a sugarcoated ending.

It's the part where we stop hiding what makes us magical.

You're not *"too much."*

You're medicine for a world running on beige.

Let's name your brilliance—on purpose.

WHAT THIS CHAPTER HELPS YOU DO

This chapter helps you harness what makes you electric.

Not by fixing your fire,

but by directing it.

You'll get rituals to protect your spark,

tools to turn passion into leadership,

and joy practices that remind you

why you were never meant to blend in.

This isn't a finish line.

It's a launchpad.

TOOL 1: HYPERFOCUS GOAL SPRINT MAP

How it was born

Here's what I learned: *my hyperfocus isn't the problem—it's the plan.*

But only when I bake in the recovery.

Now I work in sprints:

• One project

• One goal

• One re-entry ritual

I set a 2-hour block.

I write like wildfire.

Then I pause: eat something, check in with Nathan, walk around the block.

Because if I don't?

I'll disappear into my screen until my nervous system is toast *(Hupfeld et al., 2019).*

How it worked for me

I used to feel like my hyperfocus was both my gift and my curse.

I could finish entire projects in one sitting, but I'd forget to eat, move, breathe.

Then I learned to harness it.

Now I build in rituals that let me return to reality—without crashing.

Hyperfocus isn't a runaway train. It's a controlled spark.

And I manage it—so it works for me.

TOOL 2: FLOW STATE SETUP & DISRUPTION SHIELD

How it was born

When I want to hit flow on purpose, I set the stage.

Here's my ADHD flow ritual:

• Clean visual space (just my laptop, one sticky note, ginger tea)

• Background music (lo-fi or Andalusian guitar—no lyrics)

• Timer for 25 minutes

• "Protection bubble" script: *"I am allowed to be unavailable for one hour. My brain deserves this."*

This isn't hyperfocus.

This is invitational focus.

A container my brain trusts.

Distractions aren't failures.

They're part of ADHD.

But I can build a fortress for my focus—and invite my brain to meet me there *(White & Shah, 2006)*.

How it worked for me

I used to think distractions were a flaw I had to fix.

But ADHD thrives in structured creative chaos.

When I set up my environment—clean space, calm music, time-limited work—

I give my brain a map.

And it actually shows up.

That ritual became a doorway to the part of me that's quietly brilliant.

TOOL 3: RESILIENCE + JOY JOURNAL

How it was born

Here's what no one tells you about being an ADHDer:

We don't just bounce back—we bounce forward.

But we forget.

Especially in the shame spirals.

So I started keeping a joy + resilience journal.

Here's what I log:

- *"Today I almost gave up. But I didn't."*

- *"I spiraled... then I made soup."*

- *"I restarted—again."*

- *"I remembered who I was."*

- *"I made someone laugh" (Regalla et al., 2019).*

How it worked for me

Resilience wasn't natural for me—I had to practice it.

The shame spirals still happen.

But now I bounce forward.

This journal became my compass,

my reminder that I don't just survive—

I adapt, restart, evolve.

It doesn't have to be pretty.

It just has to be honest.

TOOL 4: STRENGTHS → CAREER BRIDGE

How it was born

By now, you've named your spark.

This is where we let it guide your path.

I used to think I had to pick one thing. Stick to it.

Climb the invisible ladder.

Then I realized: *I'm not a ladder person.*

I'm a trampoline person.

I bounce. I leap. I learn in loops.

So I asked:

- What energizes me?

- What lets me start, not just maintain?

- When do I feel most alive?

Then I built my work around that *(Verheul et al., 2016).*

How it worked for me

There was a time I tried to follow a linear path.

But I don't do linear.

I do spirals. Bursts. Leaps.

I built a career that works with my brain.

And for the first time—*success feels like mine.*

TOOL 5: CREATIVE CONFIDENCE REFRAME DECK

How it was born

Every time I think, *"I'm behind,"* I pull out a sticky note that says:

- *"Late bloomers bloom bigger."*

- *"Your weird is your currency."*

- *"You're not off track. You're off-grid."*

- *"This isn't too much. It's brilliance in motion."*

I leave them on my desk. In my purse. On my fridge.

These aren't affirmations.

They're truth notes *(Shaw et al., 2014)*.

How it worked for me

I tried for years to fit the mold.

Shrink my spark. Tone it down.

Turns out—that spark is the whole point.

These notes became a portal back to my true self.

Now I don't refine myself.

I release myself.

TRY THIS IF...

• Your ideas come faster than your schedule can hold them

• You've been told you're "too much" more than once

• You built an entire business on Post-its and espresso

• You've ever cried over your own idea—because it finally felt like you

• You're done shrinking to fit someone else's idea of "success"

GENTLE PRACTICE PROMPT

Tonight, write this on a note by your bed:

"My fire isn't the problem.

It's the signal."

Then thank your brain for what it created today—

even if it's just this page.

WHAT'S NEXT

This is it. The exhale after the climb.

You've named your fire.

You've mapped your rhythm.

You've loved the parts of yourself they told you to hide.

So now what?

Now, you live it.

Not perfectly. Not every day.

But truthfully. Loudly. Softly.

In playlists and phone reminders.

In "Oops I forgot" texts and "I started a thing at 2 a.m." brilliance.

You're not a problem to solve.

You're a revolution in motion.

From here on out—

Your systems will be yours.

Your pace will be yours.

Your story will be yours.

Go be your favorite version of your ADHD self.

Not fixed. Just free.

Shine, my love. The world's been waiting.

BUT IF THE FIRE DIMMERS...

If your cape's in the laundry.

If your brain's on 3%.

If your system feels far away and your spark feels buried—

Turn the page.

I made you something soft for those days.

BONUS CHAPTER: WHEN THE CAPE COMES OFF

EVERYDAY SUPPORT FOR YOUR
ADHD SUPERPOWER IN REAL LIFE

THIS ISN'T A LIST OF FIXES

It's a list of things I've lived—

and what helped when nothing else did.

Read it like a friend.

Use it like a flashlight.

Come back whenever you forget that your brain isn't broken—

it's just beautifully different.

1. I can't start—even though I really want to.

It's not willpower.

It's a missing ignition key.

Try a Two-Minute Launcher.

Try saying one sentence out loud.

Try letting someone sit nearby while you begin.

2. I get hyperfocused and forget I have a body.

You don't need a productivity hack.

You need a gentle return.

Set 90-minute "check-back-in" timers.

Anchor breaks to snacks or movement.

Give your hyperfocus a soft landing.

3. I only focus when something's exciting or urgent.

If it's boring, it might as well not exist.

Pair it with dopamine.

Turn it into a sprint.

Or ask, *"Why does this matter to Future Me?"*

4. I forget everything—even the stuff I care about.

You're not careless.

Your memory is just loud with other things.

Say it out loud.

Write it where your eyes go.

Use double alarms and habit pairings.

5. I'm surrounded by clutter I can't seem to clear.

Not lazy. Not messy. Just flooded.

Try the One-Touch Rule.

Use a "Later Bin" that actually has a date.

Let your space support your brain.

6. My emotions go from 0 to 100 in seconds.

You're not dramatic.

You're sensitive—and beautifully wired.

Name what you feel.

Take the opposite action.

Write the storm down before it sweeps you up.

7. I pretend I'm fine even when I'm drowning.

Masking kept you safe. But it's exhausting.

Track when you vanish.

Name what it costs.

Then practice showing up one layer closer to true.

8. I say yes too fast and regret it later.

You want to help. You want to be liked.

But you're left with nothing for yourself.

Say, "Let me check my schedule."

Protect a day just for rest.

Have a default "no" that feels kind and true.

9. My energy shifts with my cycle—and no one warned me.

You're not inconsistent.

You're cycling.

And your ADHD follows the tide.

Track your energy.

Plan for the peaks.

Rest during the valleys.

You're not lazy—you're syncing.

10. I feel like I'm behind everyone else.

They're thriving. You're rebooting—again.

Comparison lies.

Track your moments, not your milestones.

Replace "behind" with "becoming."

11. I miss deadlines until they're emergencies.

Not because you don't care—

but because time is fog.

Break it into sub-deadlines.

Fake urgency.

Tell someone.

Let your fear of disappointing them keep you moving.

12. I can't fall asleep—my brain won't stop spinning.

It's not insomnia.

It's a system that forgot how to slow.

Use a wind-down ritual.

No blue light. Same playlist. Same socks.

Tiny cues that whisper: you can soften now.

13. I switch tasks like wading through molasses.

Your brain doesn't jump—it lingers.

Use bridge tasks.

Stretch. Change lighting.

Give your mind time to let go before it moves on.

14. I feel like my weirdness makes me unworthy.

You were told to tone it down.

But your intensity is not the problem—

it's the point.

Tape a mantra to your mirror.

Write the wins they didn't see.

Let your weird be your why.

15. I've tried everything. Some days, nothing works.

That doesn't mean you failed.

It means you're human.

Pick your Minimum Viable Day.

Eat something. Move a little.

Rest without guilt.

You don't need to win.

You just need to begin again.

TRY THIS

Don't aim to master all 15.

Pick one. Breathe with it.

Let the others wait until you need them.

ADHD isn't solved—

it's supported.

And you're allowed to be supported softly.

THE TAKEAWAY

You're not failing at being consistent.

You're building a system that fits a brain in motion.

These tools aren't about changing who you are.

They're about making space for who you've always been.

You don't have to do it all today.

You just have to stay with yourself.

That's enough.

WRAPPING UP PART THREE: THE TOOLS THAT TURNED THE TIDE

EMPOWERING YOUR ADHD SUPERPOWER

YOU MADE IT

Every chapter, every tool, every messy, beautiful truth—

it brought you closer to yourself.

We started by naming the chaos.

The spirals.

The myths.

The lies.

And now?

We celebrate what was always underneath:

The brilliance.

The depth.

The untamed, electric, no-one-else-would-think-of-that kind of mind.

This wasn't about fixing anything.

It was about finding what already works—

and building with it.

WHAT YOU JUST DID

You didn't just collect tools.

You rebuilt your framework.

One insight, one system, one nervous-system-friendly ritual at a time.

You let go of:

• The "shoulds"

• The guilt

• The endless productivity shame spiral

And you stepped into:

• Rhythm

• Permission

• Self-leadership

You learned that ADHD isn't a glitch.

It's Brain 2.0—

the next wave of how humans move, feel, create, and connect.

It's nonlinear.

It's alive.

It's yours.

THE REALITY OF ADHD: BRAIN 2.0

ADHD isn't a flaw.

It's not a trend.

It's not a punchline.

It's a neurotype.

A way of thinking, feeling, creating, and connecting that defies straight lines.

Your brain doesn't move in rows—

it blooms in spirals.

You've seen what this means:

• Faster pattern recognition

• More intuitive leaps

• Deeper emotional resonance

• A non-linear timeline that actually works—for you

You're not behind.

You're wired for the kind of world that's fast, dynamic, and unpredictable.

You're not broken.

You're evolving.

And the world is just starting to catch up.

YOUR JOURNEY: FROM STRUGGLE TO STRENGTH

This wasn't a journey of fixing.

It was one of remembering.

You thought you were:

• Too much

• Too loud

• Too scattered

• Not enough

• Not disciplined

• Not consistent

But now you know:

• You're not inconsistent—you're cyclical

• You're not lazy—you're dopamine-deprived

• You're not chaotic—you're creative

And now, you have tools:

• The Strengths & Struggles Map

- Your ADHD Flavor

- The Dopamine Compass

- The Sensory Setup

- The Script Sets

- The Flow Anchors

You've stopped forcing your brain into someone else's system—

and started designing your own.

This is the shift:

From shame to rhythm.

From spiraling to strategy.

From *"what's wrong with me?"* to *"what works for me?"*

THE POWER OF BEING UNAPOLOGETICALLY YOU

This is the part where you stop apologizing.

For how you think.

For how you feel.

For how loud, sensitive, distracted, or intense you are.

Because that "too muchness"?

That is the signal.

The medicine.

The gift.

The revolution.

You are the person who:

• Sees what others miss

• Starts where others stall

• Brings color where there was grey

• Connects dots across galaxies

Your ADHD isn't something to shrink.

It's something to *own*.

Not everyone will get it.

That's okay.

You do.

And that changes everything.

THE ADHDer CREATIVE FORCE

So... what now?

Now, you build.

Now, you lead.

Now, you take your clarity, your courage, and your compassion—

and turn it into momentum.

Every "flaw" is just a doorway to a new tool.

Every "failure" is feedback.

Every "distraction" is data.

You were never made for the old systems.

You're here to create the new ones.

This is your spark.

This is your path.

This is your permission to lead with your wiring—

not against it.

And you've got this.

Because it's already in you.

It always has been.

CLOSING: THE FINAL REVELATION

This is what the revolution looks like—

not in loud declarations, but in quiet ownership.

No more shrinking.

No more explaining.

No more waiting to be validated.

You are the architect.

The designer.

The innovator.

The force.

And ADHD?

It's not the obstacle.

It's the origin.

You are Brain 2.0.

And this?

This is your time.

A LOVE LETTER TO THE REST OF THE WORLD

WE WERE NEVER TOO MUCH, NEVER NOT ENOUGH

DEAR NEUROTYPICALS

What It's Like to Live With ADHD — and Love From Inside It

Gather 'round.

Because I'm about to spill the ADHD tea.

Imagine me, waving a neon sign that says: **DIFFERENT OPERATING SYSTEM.**

That's exactly what this is.

I didn't get diagnosed until I was 42.

But the signs?

They've been with me since I was a kid—masked, misunderstood, mislabeled.

I'm not alone.

Globally, around 8% of children and adolescents live with ADHD *(Ayano et al., 2023)*.

And for about 2.58% of adults, ADHD doesn't fade with age—

it persists.

That number? It represents adults who still meet the full diagnostic criteria for ADHD—

with symptoms that began in childhood and never let go *(Song et al., 2021)*.

For many of us, the signs were always there.

Masked. Misunderstood. Missed.

We weren't broken.

We were just running a different operating system from the start.

Our brains weren't built for business-as-usual.

And honestly?

That might be our greatest strength.

We run on wiring that breaks rules.

That defies neat rows and rigid timelines.

That throws a dance party in our head...

and sometimes crashes mid-song.

SO, DEAR NEUROTYPICALS—

Teachers raising eyebrows when we doodle mid-lecture.

Parents groaning at cereal bowls in the bathtub (yes, we had a reason).

Bosses begging for Excel when we give them a napkin sketch.

Best friends texting "hello??" when we wander mid-conversation.

A LOVE LETTER TO THE REST OF THE WORLD

Partners wondering if we're still listening

(we are—just also thinking about moss ecosystems, sorry).

This letter's for you.

THE ADHD OPERATING SYSTEM: A CRASH COURSE

• Executive Function

You see "due dates."

We see "do-it-later-or-all-at-once" days.

Structured planning? Not our strong suit.

But last-minute brilliance?

We got that *(Willcutt et al., 2005).*

• Structural Brain Differences

Our prefrontal cortex, cerebellum,

and other regions do things... differently.

Forgetting why we walked into a room?

Not rudeness. Just neurology *(Shaw et al., 2013).*

• Cortical Maturation

Our brains develop on their own timeline.

It's not immaturity. It's delayed wiring—

and it shows in emotion, focus,

and self-control *(Shaw et al., 2013).*

• Dopamine Regulation

Imagine a golden retriever puppy chasing shiny things.

That's our dopamine.

We crave novelty, thrive on reward,

and crash without it *(Volkow et al., 2011)*.

• Inhibitory Control

Your brain has a bouncer at the door.

Ours? Takes frequent smoke breaks.

We interrupt. We impulse-buy. We overshare.

We mean well *(Nigg, 2001)*.

• Default Mode Network (DMN)

When your brain idles, it rests.

Ours spins.

We daydream in technicolor, even when we're "focusing."

It's chaos—but it's also creativity *(Metin et al., 2015)*.

• Reward Sensitivity

We don't just like adrenaline—we chase it.

Sometimes that makes us electric in a crisis.

Sometimes it derails us at 2 a.m. *(Plichta et al., 2009)*.

• Neural Connectivity

Our brains are spaghetti. Tangled. Messy. Glorious.

We might lose our phone...

but come back with a business plan *(Liston et al., 2011)*.

• Sensory Processing

We feel the world louder.

Clothing tags can wreck our day.

Lights can make us flinch.

But movies? We taste them *(Dellapiazza et al., 2021)*.

• Emotional Regulation

We don't do "mild."

We cry, rage, laugh, and love in high-def.

Our volume goes to 11—because it has to *(Shaw et al., 2014)*.

THE DAILY REALITY — A LITTLE "TOO MUCH," A LOT OF HEART

Parent–Child Tango

We forget the chore, but build a rocket from the pieces.

You're annoyed.

We're misunderstood.

And still—there's love.

Teacher–Student Rollercoaster

We're not zoning out.

We're inventing.

We're imagining.

Give us a standing desk and a flex deadline—

we'll blow your mind.

Coworkers & Cubicles

We bounce. We blurt.

We brainstorm better standing up.

Our chaos?

It can light the whole project on fire (the good kind).

Friends & Social Shenanigans

We ghost mid-text.

We forget the party.

But when we show up?

We bring every color in the box.

Intimate Relationships

We miss the reservation but write you 3 a.m. love notes.

It's not inconsistency.

It's intensity.

It's how we love—wildly, deeply, presently.

Birthdays, WhatsApp & Vanishing Acts

If we leave your message on read or skip your birthday—

it's not personal.

We just got hijacked by the mental carnival.

Voice notes help.

So does grace.

WE'RE NOT LESS — WE'RE JUST DIFFERENT

We're not broken.

We're not flaky.

We're not inconsiderate.

We're a neon swirl in a fluorescent world.

We burn bright.

Sometimes out.

But always with heart.

To everyone walking a different path—thank you.

For your patience.

For your curiosity.

And for maybe seeing that our chaos contains something rare:

Unfiltered magic.

With neon-bright sincerity,

#DearLittleMeAndOurADHD

BECAUSE FACTS MATTER: THE SCIENCE BEHIND THE SWIRL

Ayano, G., Demelash, S., Gizachew, Y., Tsegay, L., & Alati, R. (2023). The global prevalence of attention deficit hyperactivity disorder in children and adolescents: An umbrella review of meta-analyses. *Journal of Affective Disorders, 339,* 860–866.

Song, P., Zha, M., Yang, Q., Zhang, Y., Li, X., & Rudan, I. (2021). The prevalence of adult attention-deficit hyperactivity disorder: A global systematic review and meta-analysis. *Journal of Global Health, 11,* 04009.

Willcutt, E. G., Doyle, A. E., Nigg, J. T., Faraone, S. V., & Pennington, B. F. (2005). Validity of the executive function theory of attention-deficit/hyperactivity disorder: A meta-analytic review. *Biological Psychiatry, 57*(11), 1336–1346.

Shaw, P., Malek, M., Watson, B., Greenstein, D., de Rossi, P., & Sharp, W. (2013). Trajectories of cerebral cortical development in childhood and adolescence and adult attention-deficit/hyperactivity disorder. *Biological Psychiatry, 74*(8), 599–606.

Volkow, N. D., Wang, G.-J., Newcorn, J. H., Kollins, S. H., Wigal, T. L., Telang, F., Fowler, J. S., Goldstein, R. Z., Klein, N., Logan, J., Wong, C., & Swanson, J. M. (2011). Motivation deficit in ADHD is associated with dysfunction of the dopamine reward pathway. *Molecular Psychiatry, 16*(11), 1147–1154.

Nigg, J. T. (2001). Is ADHD a disinhibitory disorder? *Psychological Bulletin, 127*(5), 571–598.

Metin, B., Krebs, R. M., Wiersema, J. R., Verguts, T., Gasthuys, R., van der Meere, J. J., Achten, E., Roeyers, H., & Sonuga-Barke, E. (2015). Dysfunctional modulation of default mode network activity in attention-deficit/hyperactivity disorder. *Journal of Abnormal Psychology, 124*(1), 208–214.

Plichta, M. M., Vasic, N., Wolf, R. C., Lesch, K.-P., Brummer, D., Jacob, C., Fallgatter, A. J., & Grön, G. (2009). Neural hyporesponsiveness and hyperresponsiveness during immediate and delayed reward processing in adult attention-deficit/hyperactivity disorder. *Biological Psychiatry, 65*(1), 7–14.

Liston, C., Cohen, M. M., Teslovich, T., Levenson, D., & Casey, B. J. (2011). Atypical prefrontal connectivity in attention-deficit/hyperactivity disorder: Pathway to disease or pathological end point? *Biological Psychiatry, 69*(12), 1168–1177.

Dellapiazza, F., Michelon, C., Vernhet, C., Muratori, F., Blanc, N., Picot, M.-C., Baghdadli, A., & ELENA Study Group. (2021). Sensory processing related to attention in children with ASD, ADHD, or typical development: Results from the ELENA cohort. *European Child and Adolescent Psychiatry, 30*(2), 283–291.

Shaw, P., Stringaris, A., Nigg, J., & Leibenluft, E. (2014). Emotion dysregulation in attention-deficit/hyperactivity disorder. *The American Journal of Psychiatry, 171*(3), 276–293.

REFERENCES PART 2

Listed in order of appearance, not
alphabetically—on purpose.

**BEFORE READING PART TWO: THE TRANSLATION YOU'VE
BEEN WAITING FOR**

Faraone, S. V., Perlis, R. H., Doyle, A. E., Smoller, J. W.,
Goralnick, J. J., Holmgren, M. A., & Sklar, P. (2005).
Molecular genetics of attention-deficit/hyperactivity disorder.
Biological Psychiatry, 57(11), 1313–1323.

Turgay, A., Goodman, D. W., Asherson, P., Lasser, R. A.,
Babcock, T. F., Pucci, M. L., & Barkley, R. A. (2012). Lifespan
persistence of ADHD: The life transition model and its
application. *Journal of Clinical Psychiatry, 73*(2), 192–201.

Pataky, M. W., Young, W. F., & Sreekumaran Nair, K. (2021).
Hormonal and metabolic changes of aging and the influence of
lifestyle modifications. *Mayo Clinic Proceedings, 96*(3), 788–
814.

American Psychiatric Association. (2013). *Diagnostic and
statistical manual of mental disorders* (5th ed.). American
Psychiatric Publishing.

Song, P., Zha, M., Yang, Q., Zhang, Y., Li, X., & Rudan, I. (2021).
The prevalence of adult attention-deficit hyperactivity disorder:
A global systematic review and meta-analysis. *Journal of Global
Health, 11*, 04009.

* * *

CHAPTER 1 REFERENCES: SO, WHAT IS ADHD, REALLY?

American Psychiatric Association. (2013). *Diagnostic and
statistical manual of mental disorders* (5th ed.). American
Psychiatric Publishing.

Mahone, E. M., & Denckla, M. B. (2017). Attention-deficit/hyperactivity disorder: A historical neuropsychological perspective. *Journal of the International Neuropsychological Society, 23*(9–10), 916–929.

Faraone, S. V., Perlis, R. H., Doyle, A. E., Smoller, J. W., Goralnick, J. J., Holmgren, M. A., & Sklar, P. (2005). Molecular genetics of attention-deficit/hyperactivity disorder. *Biological Psychiatry, 57*(11), 1313-1323.

Song, P., Zha, M., Yang, Q., Zhang, Y., Li, X., & Rudan, I. (2021). The prevalence of adult attention-deficit hyperactivity disorder: A global systematic review and meta-analysis. *Journal of Global Health, 11*, 04009.

Barkley, R. A. (1997). Behavioral inhibition, sustained attention, and executive functions: Constructing a unifying theory of ADHD. *Psychological Bulletin, 121*(1), 65–94.

Ashinoff, B. K., & Abu-Akel, A. (2021). Hyperfocus: The forgotten frontier of attention. *Psychological Research, 85*(1), 1–19.

Arnsten, A. F. T. (2009). The emerging neurobiology of attention-deficit/hyperactivity disorder: The key role of the prefrontal association cortex. *Journal of Pediatrics, 154*(5), I–S43.

* * *

CHAPTER 2 REFERENCES: THE MANY FLAVORS OF ADHD

American Psychiatric Association. (2013). *Diagnostic and statistical manual of mental disorders* (5th ed.). American Psychiatric Publishing.

Creque, C. A., & Willcutt, E. G. (2021). Sluggish cognitive tempo and neuropsychological functioning. *Research on Child and Adolescent Psychopathology, 49*(8), 1001–1013.

Biederman, J., Petty, C. R., Monuteaux, M. C., Fried, R., Doyle, A. E., Seidman, L. J., & Faraone, S. V. (2010). Adult psychiatric outcomes of girls with ADHD: 11-year follow-up. *The American Journal of Psychiatry, 167*(4), 409–417.

* * *

CHAPTER 3 REFERENCES: INSIDE THE ADHD BRAIN

Volkow, N. D., Wang, G.-J., Kollins, S. H., Wigal, T. L., Newcorn, J. H., Telang, F., Fowler, J. S., Zhu, W., Logan, J., & Swanson, J. M. (2009). Evaluating dopamine reward pathway in ADHD: Clinical implications. *JAMA, 302*(10), 1084–1091.

Arnsten, A. F. T. (2009). Stress signaling pathways that impair prefrontal cortex structure and function. *Nature Reviews Neuroscience, 10*(6), 410–422.

Shaw, P., Eckstrand, K., Sharp, W., Blumenthal, J., Lerch, J. P., Greenstein, D., Clasen, L., Evans, A., Giedd, J., & Rapoport, J. L. (2007). Attention-deficit/hyperactivity disorder is characterized by a delay in cortical maturation. *Proceedings of the National Academy of Sciences, 104*(49), 19649–19654.

Castellanos, F. X., & Proal, E. (2011). Large-scale brain systems in ADHD: Beyond the prefrontal–striatal model. *Trends in Cognitive Sciences, 16*(1), 17–26.

Gkougka, D., Mitropoulos, K., Tzanakaki, G., Panagouli, E., Psaltopoulou, T., Thomaidis, L., Tsolia, M., Sergentanis, T. N., & Tsitsika, A. (2022). Gut microbiome and attention deficit/hyperactivity disorder: A systematic review. *Pediatric Research, 92*(6), 1507–1519.

* * *

CHAPTER 4 REFERENCES: EXECUTIVE DYSFUNCTION

Weigard, A., Heathcote, A., Matzke, D., & Huang-Pollock, C. (2019). Cognitive modeling suggests that attentional failures drive longer stop-signal reaction time estimates in attention deficit/hyperactivity disorder. *Clinical Psychological Science, 7*(4), 856–872.

Barkley, R. A. (1997). Attention-deficit/hyperactivity disorder, self-regulation, and time: Toward a more comprehensive theory. *Journal of Developmental and Behavioral Pediatrics, 18*(4), 271–279.

Martinussen, R., Hayden, J., Hogg-Johnson, S., & Tannock, R. (2005). A meta-analysis of working memory impairments in children with attention-deficit/hyperactivity disorder. *Journal of the American Academy of Child & Adolescent Psychiatry, 44*(4), 377–384.

Castellanos, F. X., Sonuga-Barke, E. J. S., Milham, M. P., & Tannock, R. (2006). Characterizing cognition in ADHD: Beyond executive dysfunction. *Trends in Cognitive Sciences, 10*(3), 117–123.

Dekkers, T. J., Agelink van Rentergem, J. A., Huizenga, H. M., Raber, H., Shoham, R., Popma, A., & Pollak, Y. (2021). Decision-making deficits in ADHD are not related to risk seeking but to suboptimal decision-making: Meta-analytical and novel experimental evidence. *Journal of Attention Disorders, 25*(4), 486–501.

van Rooij, D., Hartman, C. A., Mennes, M., Oosterlaan, J., Franke, B., Rommelse, N., Heslenfeld, D., Faraone, S. V., Buitelaar, J. K., & Hoekstra, P. J. (2015). Altered neural connectivity during response inhibition in adolescents with attention-deficit/hyperactivity disorder and their unaffected siblings. *NeuroImage: Clinical, 7*, 325–335.

* * *

CHAPTER 5 REFERENCES: HORMONES AND ADHD

Weetman, A. P. (2000). Graves' disease. *The New England Journal of Medicine, 343*(17), 1236–1248.

Arnsten, A. F. T. (2009). Stress signalling pathways that impair prefrontal cortex structure and function. *Nature Reviews Neuroscience, 10*(6), 410–422.

Eng, A. G., Nirjar, U., Elkins, A. R., Sizemore, Y. J., Monticello, K. N., Petersen, M. K., Miller, S. A., Barone, J., Eisenlohr-Moul, T. A., & Martel, M. M. (2024). Attention-deficit/hyperactivity disorder and the menstrual cycle: Theory and evidence. *Hormones and Behavior, 158*, 105466.

Martel, M. M., Klump, K., Nigg, J. T., Breedlove, S. M., & Sisk, C. L. (2009). Potential hormonal mechanisms of attention-deficit/hyperactivity disorder and major depressive disorder: A new perspective. *Hormones and Behavior, 55*(4), 465–479.

Zhu, D. F., Wang, Z. X., Zhang, D. R., Pan, Z. L., He, S., Hu, X., Chen, X. C., & Zhou, J. N. (2006). fMRI revealed neural substrate for reversible working memory dysfunction in subclinical hypothyroidism. *Brain, 129*(11), 2923–2930.

Young, S., Adamo, N., Ásgeirsdóttir, B. B., Branney, P., Beckett, M., Colley, W., Cubbin, S., Deeley, Q., Farrag, E., Gudjonsson, G., Hill, P., Hollingdale, J., Kilic, O., Lloyd, T., Mason, P., Paliokosta, E., Perecherla, S., Sedgwick, J., Skirrow, C., Tierney, K., van Rensburg, K., & Woodhouse, E. (2020). Females with ADHD: An expert consensus statement taking a lifespan approach providing guidance for the identification and treatment of attention-deficit/hyperactivity disorder in girls and women. *BMC Psychiatry, 20*(1), 404.

* * *

CHAPTER 6 REFERENCES: EMOTIONAL & SENSORY DYSREGULATION

Shaw, P., Stringaris, A., Nigg, J., & Leibenluft, E. (2014). Emotion dysregulation in attention deficit hyperactivity disorder. *The American Journal of Psychiatry, 171*(3), 276–293.

Bondü, R., & Esser, G. (2015). Justice and rejection sensitivity in children and adolescents with ADHD symptoms. *European Child & Adolescent Psychiatry, 24*(2), 185–198.

Barkley, R. A., & Fischer, M. (2010). The unique contribution of emotional impulsiveness to impairment in major life activities in hyperactive children as adults. *Journal of the American Academy of Child & Adolescent Psychiatry, 49*(5), 503–513.

Porges, S. W. (2007). The polyvagal perspective. *Biological Psychology, 74*(2), 116–143.

Faraone, S. V., Biederman, J., Spencer, T., Wilens, T., Seidman, L. J., Mick, E., & Doyle, A. E. (2000). Attention-deficit/hyperactivity disorder in adults: An overview. *Biological Psychiatry, 48*(1), 9–20.

* * *

CHAPTER 7 REFERENCES: ADHD IN REAL LIFE

Del Campo, N., Chamberlain, S. R., Sahakian, B. J., & Robbins, T. W. (2011). The roles of dopamine and noradrenaline in the pathophysiology and treatment of attention-deficit/hyperactivity disorder. *Biological Psychiatry, 69*(12), e145–e157.

Capuozzo, A., Rizzato, S., Grossi, G., & Strappini, F. (2024). A systematic review on social cognition in ADHD: The role of language, theory of mind, and executive functions. *Brain Sciences, 14*(11), 1117.

Willcutt, E. G., Doyle, A. E., Nigg, J. T., Faraone, S. V., & Pennington, B. F. (2005). Validity of the executive function theory of attention-deficit/hyperactivity disorder: A meta-analytic review. *Biological Psychiatry, 57*(11), 1336–1346.

Shaw, P., Stringaris, A., Nigg, J., & Leibenluft, E. (2014). Emotion dysregulation in attention deficit hyperactivity disorder. *The American Journal of Psychiatry, 171*(3), 276–293.

Surman, C. B. H., Biederman, J., Spencer, T., Miller, C. A., McDermott, K. M., & Faraone, S. V. (2013). Understanding deficient emotional self-regulation in adults with attention deficit hyperactivity disorder: A controlled study. *Attention Deficit and Hyperactivity Disorders, 5*(3), 273–281.

Corominas-Roso, M., Palomar, G., Ferrer, R., Real, A., Nogueira, M., Corrales, M., Casas, M., & Ramos-Quiroga, J. A. (2015). Cortisol response to stress in adults with attention deficit hyperactivity disorder. *International Journal of Neuropsychopharmacology, 18*(9), pyv027.

Russell, A. E., Ford, T., Williams, R., & Russell, G. (2016). The association between socioeconomic disadvantage and attention deficit/hyperactivity disorder (ADHD): A systematic review. *Child Psychiatry & Human Development, 47*(3), 440–458.

* * *

CHAPTER 8 REFERENCES: SLEEP, SUBSTANCES & SELF-MEDICATION

Coogan, A. N., & McGowan, N. M. (2017). A systematic review of circadian function, chronotype and chronotherapy in attention-deficit/hyperactivity disorder. *Attention Deficit and Hyperactivity Disorders, 9*(3), 129-147.

Sobanski, E., Schredl, M., Kettler, N., & Alm, B. (2008). Sleep in adults with attention deficit hyperactivity disorder (ADHD) before and during treatment with methylphenidate: A controlled polysomnographic study. *Sleep, 31*(3), 375-381.

van Andel, E., Bijlenga, D., Vogel, S. W. N., Beekman, A. T. F., & Kooij, J. J. S. (2021). Effects of chronotherapy on circadian rhythm and ADHD symptoms in adults with attention-deficit/hyperactivity disorder and delayed sleep phase syndrome: A randomized clinical trial. *Chronobiology International, 38*(2), 260-269.

Fargason, R. E., Fobian, A. D., Hablitz, L. M., Paul, J. R., White, B. A., Cropsey, K. L., & Gamble, K. L. (2017). Correcting delayed circadian phase with bright light therapy predicts improvement in ADHD symptoms: A pilot study. *Journal of Psychiatric Research, 91*, 105-110.

Del Campo, N., Chamberlain, S. R., Sahakian, B. J., & Robbins, T. W. (2011). The roles of dopamine and noradrenaline in the pathophysiology and treatment of attention-deficit/hyperactivity disorder. *Biological Psychiatry, 69*(12), e145-e157.

Lee, S. S., Humphreys, K. L., Flory, K., Liu, R., & Glass, K. (2011). Prospective association of childhood attention-deficit/hyperactivity disorder (ADHD) and substance use and abuse/dependence: A meta-analytic review. *Clinical Psychology Review, 31*(3), 328-341.

* * *

CHAPTER 9 REFERENCES: ADHD & CO-OCCURRING CONDITIONS

Stein, D. J., Koenen, K. C., Friedman, M. J., Hill, E., McLaughlin, K. A., Petukhova, M., & Kessler, R. C. (2013). Dissociation in posttraumatic stress disorder: Evidence from the World Mental Health Surveys. *Biological Psychiatry, 73*(4), 302-312.

D'Agati, E., Curatolo, P., & Mazzone, L. (2019). Comorbidity between ADHD and anxiety disorders across the lifespan. *International Journal of Psychiatry in Clinical Practice, 23*(4), 238-244.

Biederman, J., Newcorn, J., & Sprich, S. (1991). Comorbidity of attention deficit hyperactivity disorder with conduct, depressive, anxiety, and other disorders. *The American Journal of Psychiatry, 148*(5), 564-577.

Craig, F., Lamanna, A. L., Margari, F., Matera, E., Simone, M., & Margari, L. (2015). Overlap between autism spectrum disorders and attention deficit hyperactivity disorder: Searching for distinctive/common clinical features. *Autism Research, 8*(3), 328-337.

Brem, S., Grünblatt, E., Drechsler, R., Riederer, P., & Walitza, S. (2014). The neurobiological link between OCD and ADHD. *ADHD Attention Deficit and Hyperactivity Disorders, 6*(3), 175-202.

Levin, R. L., & Rawana, J. S. (2016). Attention-deficit/hyperactivity disorder and eating disorders across the lifespan: A systematic review of the literature. *Clinical Psychology Review, 50*, 22-36.

* * *

CHAPTER 10 REFERENCES: ADHD IS REAL. LET'S KILL THE MYTHS

Turgay, A., Goodman, D. W., Asherson, P., Lasser, R. A., Babcock, T., Pucci, M. L., & Barkley, R. A. (2012). Lifespan persistence of ADHD: The life transition model and its application. *Journal of Clinical Psychiatry, 73*(2), 192-201.

Beaton, D. M., Sirois, F., & Milne, E. (2022). Experiences of criticism in adults with ADHD: A qualitative study. *PLOS ONE*, *17*(2), e0263366.

Sonuga-Barke, E. J. S., Brandeis, D., Cortese, S., Daley, D., Ferrin, M., Holtmann, M., & Sergeant, J. (2013). Nonpharmacological interventions for ADHD: Systematic review and meta-analyses of RCTs of dietary and psychological treatments. *American Journal of Psychiatry, 170*(3), 275–289.

Quinn, P. O., & Madhoo, M. (2014). A review of attention-deficit/hyperactivity disorder in women and girls: Uncovering this hidden diagnosis. *Primary Care Companion for CNS Disorders, 16*(3), PCC.13r01596.

Song, P., Zha, M., Yang, Q., Zhang, Y., Li, X., & Rudan, I. (2021). The prevalence of adult attention-deficit hyperactivity disorder: A global systematic review and meta-analysis. *Journal of Global Health, 11*, 04009.

* * *

CHAPTER 11 REFERENCES: ADHD IS ALSO A SUPERPOWER

White, H. A., & Shah, P. (2006). Uninhibited imaginations: Creativity in adults with Attention-Deficit/Hyperactivity Disorder. *Personality and Individual Differences, 40*(6), 1121–1131.

Hupfeld, K. E., Abagis, T. R., & Shah, P. (2019). Living "in the zone": Hyperfocus in adult ADHD. *ADHD Attention Deficit and Hyperactivity Disorders, 11*(2), 191–208.

Regalla, M. A. R., Segenreich, D., Guilherme, P. R., & Mattos, P. (2019). Resilience levels among adolescents with ADHD using quantitative measures in a family-design study. *Trends in Psychiatry and Psychotherapy, 41*(3), 262–267.

Shaw, P., Stringaris, A., Nigg, J., & Leibenluft, E. (2014). Emotion dysregulation in attention deficit hyperactivity disorder. *The American Journal of Psychiatry, 171*(3), 276–293.

Beaton, D. M., Sirois, F., & Milne, E. (2022). Experiences of criticism in adults with ADHD: A qualitative study. *PLOS ONE*, *17*(2), e0263366.

Verheul, I., Rietdijk, W., Block, J., Franken, I., Larsson, H., &

Thurik, R. (2016). The association between attention-deficit/hyperactivity (ADHD) symptoms and self-employment. *European Journal of Epidemiology, 31*(8), 793–801.

REFERENCES PART 3

Listed in order of appearance, not alphabetically—on purpose.

CHAPTER 1 REFERENCES: STRENGTHS & STRUGGLES MAPPING

Hallowell, E. M., & Ratey, J. J. (2021). *ADHD 2.0: New science and essential strategies for thriving with distraction—from childhood through adulthood.* Ballantine Books.

Barkley, R. A. (1997). *Behavioral inhibition, sustained attention, and executive functions: Constructing a unifying theory of ADHD. Psychological Bulletin, 121*(1), 65–94.

Volkow, N. D., Wang, G.-J., Kollins, S. H., Wigal, T. L., Newcorn, J. H., Telang, F., Fowler, J. S., Zhu, W., Logan, J., & Swanson, J. M. (2009). *Evaluating dopamine reward pathway in ADHD: Clinical implications. JAMA, 302*(10), 1084–1091.

Sarkis, S. M. (2015). *Natural relief for adult ADHD: Complementary strategies for increasing focus, attention, and motivation with or without medication.* New Harbinger Publications.

Mahone, E. M., & Denckla, M. B. (2017). *Attention-deficit/hyperactivity disorder: A historical neuropsychological perspective. Journal of the International Neuropsychological Society, 23*(9–10), 916–929.

* * *

CHAPTER 2 REFERENCES: FLAVOR-SPECIFIC STRATEGIES

Fassbender, C., Krafft, C. E., & Schweitzer, J. B. (2015). *Differentiating SCT and inattentive symptoms in ADHD using fMRI measures of cognitive control. NeuroImage: Clinical, 8,* 390–397.

Willcutt, E. G. (2012). *The prevalence of DSM-IV attention-*

deficit/hyperactivity disorder: A meta-analytic review. *Neurotherapeutics, 9*(3), 490–499.

Biederman, J., Petty, C. R., Monuteaux, M. C., Fried, R., Doyle, A. E., Seidman, L. J., & Faraone, S. V. (2010). *Adult psychiatric outcomes of girls with ADHD: 11-year follow-up. The American Journal of Psychiatry, 167*(4), 409–417.

Puyjarinet, F., Bégel, V., Lopez, R., Dellacherie, D., & Dalla Bella, S. (2017). *Children and adults with Attention-Deficit/Hyperactivity Disorder cannot move to the beat. Scientific Reports, 7*(1), 11550.

Slobodin, O., & Davidovitch, M. (2019). *Gender differences in objective and subjective measures of ADHD among clinic-referred children. Frontiers in Human Neuroscience, 13*, 441.

Lane, S. J., & Reynolds, S. (2019). *Sensory over-responsivity as an added dimension in ADHD. Frontiers in Integrative Neuroscience, 13*, 40.

Blanchfield, T. (2023, December 13). *Types of therapy for ADHD.* Verywell Mind.

* * *

CHAPTER 3 REFERENCES: FUEL, FLOW & FOCUS

Fargason, R. E., Fobian, A. D., Hablitz, L. M., Paul, J. R., White, B. A., Cropsey, K. L., & Gamble, K. L. (2017). Correcting delayed circadian phase with bright light therapy predicts improvement in ADHD symptoms: A pilot study. *Journal of Psychiatric Research, 91*, 105–110.

Ratey, J. J. (2024, December 4). The ADHD exercise solution. *ADDitude Magazine.*

Morgan, K. K. (2024, September 2). Amino acids for ADHD. *WebMD.*

Levy Schwartz, M., Magzal, F., Yehuda, I., & Tamir, S. (2024). Exploring the impact of probiotics on adult ADHD management through a double-blind RCT. *Scientific Reports, 14*(1), 26830.

Arnsten, A. F. T. (2009). The emerging neurobiology of attention deficit hyperactivity disorder: The key role of the prefrontal association cortex. *Journal of Pediatrics, 154*(5 Suppl), I–S43.

REFERENCES PART 3

Volkow, N. D., Wang, G.-J., Kollins, S. H., Wigal, T. L., Newcorn, J. H., Telang, F., Fowler, J. S., Zhu, W., Logan, J., & Swanson, J. M. (2009). Evaluating dopamine reward pathway in ADHD: Clinical implications. *JAMA, 302*(10), 1084-1091.

Shier, A. C., Reichenbacher, T., Ghuman, H. S., & Ghuman, J. K. (2012). *Pharmacological treatment of attention deficit hyperactivity disorder in children and adolescents: Clinical strategies. Journal of Central Nervous System Diseases, 5*, 1-17.

Volkow, N. D., & Swanson, J. M. (2013). Clinical practice: Adult attention deficit-hyperactivity disorder. *The New England Journal of Medicine, 369*(20), 1935-1944.

* * *

CHAPTER 4 REFERENCES: LAUNCH SEQUENCE INTERRUPTED

Weigard, A., Heathcote, A., Matzke, D., & Huang-Pollock, C. (2019). Cognitive modeling suggests that attentional failures drive longer stop-signal reaction time estimates in attention deficit/hyperactivity disorder. *Clinical Psychological Science, 7*(4), 856-872.

Barkley, R. A. (1997). *ADHD and the nature of self-control.* The Guilford Press.

Castellanos, F. X., Sonuga-Barke, E. J. S., Milham, M. P., & Tannock, R. (2006). Characterizing cognition in ADHD: Beyond executive dysfunction. *Trends in Cognitive Sciences, 10*(3), 117-123.

Martinussen, R., Hayden, J., Hogg-Johnson, S., & Tannock, R. (2005). A meta-analysis of working memory impairments in children with attention-deficit/hyperactivity disorder. *Journal of the American Academy of Child and Adolescent Psychiatry, 44*(4), 377-384.

Cleveland Clinic. (2025, January 6). *What is 'body doubling' and can it help with ADHD?* Cleveland Clinic Health Essentials.

* * *

CHAPTER 5 REFERENCES: HORMONES & THE ADHD BODY

Roberts, B., Eisenlohr-Moul, T., & Martel, M. M. (2018). Reproductive steroids and ADHD symptoms across the menstrual cycle. *Psychoneuroendocrinology, 88,* 105–114.

Grigorova, M., & Sherwin, B. B. (2012). Thyroid hormones and cognitive functioning in healthy, euthyroid women: A correlational study. *Hormones and Behavior, 61*(4), 617–622.

Arnsten, A. F. T. (2009). The emerging neurobiology of attention deficit hyperactivity disorder: The key role of the prefrontal association cortex. *Journal of Pediatrics, 154*(5 Suppl), I–S43.

Young, S., Adamo, N., Ásgeirsdóttir, B. B., Branney, P., Beckett, M., Colley, W., & Woodhouse, E. (2020). Females with ADHD: An expert consensus statement taking a lifespan approach providing guidance for the identification and treatment of attention-deficit/hyperactivity disorder in girls and women. *BMC Psychiatry, 20*(1), 404.

* * *

CHAPTER 6 REFERENCES: EMOTIONAL THUNDER & SENSORY STORMS

Linehan, M. M. (1993). *Cognitive-behavioral treatment of borderline personality disorder.* Guilford Press.

Porges, S. W. (2007). The polyvagal perspective. *Biological Psychology, 74*(2), 116–143.

Clément, M.-A., Lee, K., Park, M., Sinn, A., & Miyake, N. (2022). The need for sensory-friendly "zones": Learning from youth on the autism spectrum, their families, and autistic mentors using a participatory approach. *Frontiers in Psychology, 13,* 883331.

Slobodin, O., & Davidovitch, M. (2019). Gender differences in objective and subjective measures of ADHD among clinic-referred children. *Frontiers in Human Neuroscience, 13,* 441.

Bondü, R., & Esser, G. (2015). Justice and rejection sensitivity in children and adolescents with ADHD symptoms. *European Child & Adolescent Psychiatry, 24*(2), 185–198.

REFERENCES PART 3

* * *

CHAPTER 7 REFERENCES: FUNCTIONING IN THE MESS

Del Campo, N., Chamberlain, S. R., Sahakian, B. J., & Robbins, T. W. (2011). The roles of dopamine and noradrenaline in the pathophysiology and treatment of attention-deficit/hyperactivity disorder. *Biological Psychiatry, 69*(12), e145–e157.

Willcutt, E. G., Doyle, A. E., Nigg, J. T., Faraone, S. V., & Pennington, B. F. (2005). Validity of the executive function theory of attention-deficit/hyperactivity disorder: A meta-analytic review. *Biological Psychiatry, 57*(11), 1336–1346.

Capuozzo, A., Rizzato, S., Grossi, G., & Strappini, F. (2024). A systematic review on social cognition in ADHD: The role of language, theory of mind, and executive functions. *Brain Sciences*, 14(11), 1117.

Surman, C. B. H., Biederman, J., Spencer, T., Miller, C. A., McDermott, K. M., & Faraone, S. V. (2013). Understanding deficient emotional self-regulation in adults with attention deficit hyperactivity disorder: A controlled study. *Attention Deficit and Hyperactivity Disorders, 5*(3), 273–281.

Ginapp, C. M., Greenberg, N. R., MacDonald-Gagnon, G., Angarita, G. A., Bold, K. W., & Potenza, M. N. (2023). "Dysregulated not deficit": A qualitative study on symptomatology of ADHD in young adults. *PLOS ONE, 18*(10), e0292721.

* * *

CHAPTER 8 REFERENCES: SLEEP, SUBSTANCES & SELF-MEDICATION

van Andel, E., Bijlenga, D., Vogel, S. W. N., Beekman, A. T. F., & Kooij, J. J. S. (2021). Effects of chronotherapy on circadian rhythm and ADHD symptoms in adults with attention-deficit/hyperactivity disorder and delayed sleep phase syndrome: A randomized clinical trial. *Chronobiology International, 38*(2), 260–269.

Fargason, R. E., Fobian, A. D., Hablitz, L. M., Paul, J. R., White, B. A., Cropsey, K. L., & Gamble, K. L. (2017). Correcting delayed circadian phase with bright light therapy predicts improvement in ADHD symptoms: A pilot study. *Journal of Psychiatric Research, 91*, 105–110.

Sobanski, E., Schredl, M., Kettler, N., & Alm, B. (2008). Sleep in adults with attention deficit hyperactivity disorder (ADHD) before and during treatment with methylphenidate: A controlled polysomnographic study. *Sleep, 31*(3), 375–381.

Del Campo, N., Chamberlain, S. R., Sahakian, B. J., & Robbins, T. W. (2011). The roles of dopamine and noradrenaline in the pathophysiology and treatment of attention-deficit/hyperactivity disorder. *Biological Psychiatry, 69*(12), e145–e157.

Coogan, A. N., & McGowan, N. M. (2017). A systematic review of circadian function, chronotype and chronotherapy in attention deficit hyperactivity disorder. *Attention Deficit and Hyperactivity Disorders, 9*(3), 129–147.

* * *

CHAPTER 9 REFERENCES: ADHD & THE REST OF THE BRAIN PARTY

D'Agati, E., Curatolo, P., & Mazzone, L. (2019). Comorbidity between ADHD and anxiety disorders across the lifespan. *International journal of psychiatry in clinical practice, 23*(4), 238–244.

Stein, D. J., Koenen, K. C., Friedman, M. J., Hill, E., McLaughlin, K. A., Petukhova, M., & Kessler, R. C. (2013). Dissociation in posttraumatic stress disorder: Evidence from the World Mental Health Surveys. *Biological Psychiatry, 73*(4), 302–312.

Abramovitch, A., Dar, R., Mittelman, A., & Wilhelm, S. (2015). Comorbidity between attention deficit/hyperactivity disorder and obsessive-compulsive disorder across the lifespan: A systematic and critical review. *Harvard Review of Psychiatry, 23*(4), 245–262.

Levin, R. L., & Rawana, J. S. (2016). Attention-deficit/hyperactivity disorder and eating disorders across the lifespan: A systematic review of the literature. *Clinical Psychology Review, 50*, 22–36.

Russell, S. T., Bishop, M. D., Saba, V. C., James, I., & Ioverno, S. (2021). Promoting school safety for LGBTQ and all students. *Policy insights from the behavioral and brain sciences*, 8(2), 160–166.

Lopez, P. L., Torrente, F. M., Ciapponi, A., Lischinsky, A. G., Cetkovich-Bakmas, M., Rojas, J. I., Romano, M., & Manes, F. F. (2018). Cognitive-behavioural interventions for attention deficit hyperactivity disorder (ADHD) in adults. *The Cochrane database of systematic reviews*, 3(3), CD010840.

* * *

CHAPTER 10 REFERENCES: ADHD IS REAL

Song, P., Zha, M., Yang, Q., Zhang, Y., Li, X., & Rudan, I. (2021). The prevalence of adult attention-deficit hyperactivity disorder: A global systematic review and meta-analysis. *Journal of Global Health, 11*, 04009.

Beaton, D. M., Sirois, F. M., & Milne, E. (2022). Experiences of criticism in adults with ADHD: A qualitative study. *PLOS ONE, 17*(2), e0263366.

Turgay, A., Goodman, D. W., Asherson, P., Lasser, R. A., Babcock, T. F., Pucci, M. L., & Barkley, R. (2012). Lifespan persistence of ADHD: The life transition model and its application. *Journal of Clinical Psychiatry, 73*(2), 192–201.

Quinn, P. O., & Madhoo, M. (2014). A review of attention-deficit/hyperactivity disorder in women and girls: Uncovering this hidden diagnosis. *Primary Care Companion for CNS Disorders, 16*(3), PCC.13r01596.

Sonuga-Barke, E. J. S., Brandeis, D., Cortese, S., Daley, D., Ferrin, M., Holtmann, M., Stevenson, J., Danckaerts, M., van der Oord, S., Döpfner, M., Dittmann, R. W., Simonoff, E., Zuddas, A., Banaschewski, T., Buitelaar, J., Coghill, D., Hollis, C., Konofal, E., Lecendreux, M., Wong, I. C. K., & Sergeant, J. (2013). Nonpharmacological interventions for ADHD: Systematic review and meta-analyses of randomized controlled trials of dietary and psychological treatments. *American Journal of Psychiatry, 170*(3), 275–289.

* * *

CHAPTER 11 REFERENCES: THE ADHD SUPERPOWER SUITE

Hupfeld, K. E., Abagis, T. R., & Shah, P. (2019). Living "in the zone": Hyperfocus in adult ADHD. *ADHD Attention Deficit and Hyperactivity Disorders, 11*(2), 191–208.

White, H. A., & Shah, P. (2006). Uninhibited imaginations: Creativity in adults with Attention-Deficit/Hyperactivity Disorder. *Personality and Individual Differences, 40*(6), 1121–1131.

Regalla, M. A. R., Segenreich, D., Guilherme, P. R., & Mattos, P. (2019). Resilience levels among adolescents with ADHD using quantitative measures in a family-design study. *Trends in Psychiatry and Psychotherapy, 41*(3), 262–267.

Verheul, I., Rietdijk, W., Block, J. H., Franken, I., Larsson, H., & Thurik, R. (2016). The association between attention-deficit/hyperactivity (ADHD) symptoms and self-employment. *European Journal of Epidemiology, 31*(8), 793–801.

Shaw, P., Stringaris, A., Nigg, J., & Leibenluft, E. (2014). Emotion dysregulation in attention deficit hyperactivity disorder. *American Journal of Psychiatry, 171*(3), 276–293.

ACKNOWLEDGMENTS

Writing this book was not a solo journey.

It was made possible by the incredible people who supported, inspired, and believed in me along the way.

To all the ADHD warriors out there—parents, children, entrepreneurs, and dreamers—who refuse to conform to society's expectations and instead forge their own paths: this book is for you.

May it remind you that you are not alone, that your mind is wired for greatness, and that your potential is limitless.

To my son, Nathan—my greatest teacher and adventure partner.

Your boundless creativity, resilience, and fearless spirit remind me every day why embracing our unique brains is the key to unlocking our true potential.

You are my superhero, and this book is as much yours as it is mine.

To my family and friends who stood by me, even when

I felt lost or overwhelmed—thank you for your patience, your love, and your unwavering belief in me.

Your support has been my anchor through the ups and downs.

And to the countless researchers, clinicians, and ADHD advocates whose work has paved the way for greater understanding and acceptance of neurodiversity:

your contributions have given people like me the tools to thrive.

I hope this book continues to spread that knowledge and empowerment.

ABOUT THE AUTHOR

Patrycja Marta Jerushalmy is an author, entrepreneur, and late-diagnosed ADHD mother who once played a mystical sorceress in *Avengers: Endgame*—but her real superpower is raising a neurodivergent son while rewriting her entire relationship with her brain.

She's lived across continents, speaks five languages, and holds a Master's in Physical Education and Pedagogy. Her path has spiraled through high-tech, education, culture, burnout, breakthroughs, and beautifully chaotic reinvention.

When her son was diagnosed, everything clicked. She dove headfirst into neuroscience, alternative healing, and trial-by-chaos learning to uncover tools that actually work—for both of them.

She is an advocate for authenticity and personal growth, helping others reclaim their truth without shame.

Dear Little Me is her manifesto: a metaphor-rich, emotionally raw, radically honest love letter to every brain that's ever been told it's too much—or not enough.

Her mission?

To help beautifully wired humans stop apologizing—and start building systems, stories, and self-trust that actually fit.

Her motto?

You were never too much—and never not enough.

And she means it.

DISCLAIMER

This book is a personal account of lived experience with Attention-Deficit/Hyperactivity Disorder (ADHD), including reflections as a late-diagnosed adult and a parent of a neurodivergent child. It is intended for informational and narrative purposes only. It does not constitute professional medical, psychological, or therapeutic advice, diagnosis, or treatment.

The author is not a licensed clinician, medical provider, psychologist, or therapist. Nothing in this book should be used as a basis for altering treatment, medication, or mental health care without direct consultation with qualified professionals. Readers are urged to use their own discretion and to consult their care teams before making any decisions related to health or mental well-being.

This material is presented "as is," without guarantees, warranties, or representations of outcomes. The author and publisher disclaim all liability for any loss, injury, harm, or consequence resulting from the use, misuse, or interpretation of the content in this book.

All references to research, studies, books, or expert commentary are included in good faith and based on the author's personal interpretation at the time of writing. Every effort has been made to cite sources accurately and within the context of the original work. However, inclusion of a citation does not imply endorsement by the original author, nor does it indicate that the cited research supports all views expressed in this book.

Any misrepresentation or misuse of a source is entirely unintentional. The author welcomes correction if any cited work has been inaccurately described. All source material remains the intellectual property of the original authors and is referenced here for commentary, reflection, and narrative support under the principles of fair use.

This book is not a manual, a diagnostic tool, or a clinical framework. It is one person's truth—offered openly, shared with care, and grounded in real life.

Patrycja Marta Jerushalmy

Author

Made in United States
Orlando, FL
08 June 2025

61939335R00252